# Intuition Routine

Patrick C. Ehler

# Dedication

I dedicate this book to every name that has ever been spoken. I dedicate it to every name I have not met while being here. I dedicate this book to you, who is spending time with these written thoughts. I dedicate this book to my grandma, a fountain of inspiration.
Grounded, caring, and devoted, giving me space to express myself and live in whatever manner. I dedicate this book to my mom who always gave me the freedom to be whom I felt like. I dedicate it to my dads, the one that was a part of my creation and the one that was a part of raising me. I dedicate this book to my brother Christian, the one who fuels all my aspirations with endless nourishment. I dedicate this book to Sandra, my sister, who supports me with endless moments of remembrance and 'unremembrance' of given moments we share together. I dedicate this book to all my

ancestors who are the reason I'm here in this body, getting my thoughts on paper. I dedicate this book to Verena, my aunt, with her pure magic which enchants my views in every encounter. I dedicate this book to the thousands of hours of laughter and tears with my dearest and beloved friend Anita, making every moment a thoughtful one. I dedicate this book to Stefan, my friend who always reminds me of where I came from and always gives me the space to explore individuality and creativity. I dedicate this book to Magick which empowered me not only to write this book but to find a mentor that supports me when I have a deep curiosity, and I found it—life itself. I dedicate this book to Lumira Weidner, a bright sun, wise, powerful, and grounded soul, lighting the fire to express myself through writing. I dedicate this book to Jana Iger always fruitful and healing in every word she 'spells.' I dedicate this book to every soul that I have had the honor to quote and name in this collection of thoughts. Last but not least, I dedicate this book to myself, to my thoughts, my present existence, my experiences, all the people that live within my heart, all that I may discover from the past, and all that may come in the future.

# Contents

# Introduction

This book is an invitation to connect to your intuition. Often intuition is something that is described as a warning feeling that's coming out of the gut. However, intuition is the always joyful inner guide to wisdom, freedom, health and peace. All warnings, concerns, worries and thoughts that lead us far away from what is really happening in front of our two eyes come from the imagination that is created through the egoic identity and with it, belief systems. The egoic identity is the quality of being and believing identically as a moment ago. It is the quality of being the same as yesterday.

Intuition always supports us in understanding and managing what it means for our individuality to be healthy, physically and emotionally.

So here the first question. Can you trust your intuition if it is bringing you to an emotional level that includes suffering through judging others and ourselves, worrying about the past and future, and resistance? Is that the intuition or maybe the mind that's playing a game and wants to fight with reality? Do those kind of negative feelings inherit the truth that intuition wants to tell us, like living in peace, freedom and health? Intuition is a truth that doesn't judge others, doesn't judge the moment and leads us to freedom of mind. It is a judgment thus it comes in freedom.

Learning to listen to your intuition is the portal to peace, the freedom from all suffering. I invite you with all of my heart to experience peace within yourself, as well as the world around you. You will find peace through this wonderful opportunity of distinguishing between the intuition and the stories created through the egoic identity that carries all belief systems. This will allow you to integrate the mind as a friend and learn how to be a lover of what is, to see reality instead of the imagination of the mind.

This book will leave you with concrete skills that will cultivate and strengthen the intuition, as well as provide practical and scientific information about what impacts general well-being, health and a flowing state of mind. Living intuitively supports general health by trusting the intuition and finding correlations between scientific and personal experiences. This book is about 'mycellf' my perspectives and momentums from daily life examples to abstract moments i had the chance to experience. This book is yes indeed about me, so don't expect to find yourcellf within it. Thus i know when you don't expect to find you may connect to the essence and the aim of this book.

Using the knowledge of science and intuitive wisdom this book provides practices for a constant connection to intuition. This book will be an intense, freeing and perspective changing experience with practical tools to use dedicated and integrated in daily life. This book will support you to understand deep and wonderful concepts that might seem more complex than they are in reality. A highly practical and accessible source to gain more knowledge on how to access your intuition, the main purpose of this book is to show that anyone with an open heart and mind can connect to their own intuitive wisdom and become inspired to learn new skills on how to cultivate intuition for a world that just flows in freedom of mind, peace and health.

# 1.   How Living Intuitively Changed My Life

During the book there will be several perspectives on how living intuitively alleviates depression and even strengthens the inner guide that leads us to joy, in situations that were once debilitating. It helps decrease stress and lessen anxiety or fear. Improving any relationship, business or personal, it supports to deepen a bond of trust, connection and intimacy with loved ones, family, friends and with yourself. Thus know words are pointers but the meaning of the truth behind this is rather a fragmented one and understanding the essence of it will come through experiencing the book. I include some personal stories that were big aha moments for me to inspire you to see where in your life it was that intense experiences had strengthened the connection to your wisdom.

Living intuitively reduces anger through understanding what makes you upset or resentful and you will become reactive less often. The reactions will have less intensity.

It shows reality as it is and gifts us with increased mental clarity, helping in any circumstance to work and live more productively, creatively and 'IntelliGently'.

Opening a space for inner peace, you will start to love reality in its totality.


N.B. All biological processes presented here are based on biomedical research and genetic studies. I include my personal experiences to make it conceptually understandable. This book's aim is to provide general information for educational purposes only. The information provided is not intended to be a substitute for medical advice or care, but an invitation to combine the intuitive wisdom with the amazing scientific findings of biomedical research.

April showers bring May flowers.

# 2. What Is Intuition

There is a high intelligence which is called intuition
and it is often just covered up behind our beliefs and the
identity we create around ourselves, specifically in the
imagination of our minds. It is only by pure intuition that
reality arrives for the mind and we can perceive peace
flooding in all that's present in real life around us.
Reality is what is in front of our eyes, in this moment,
right now, and intuition leads us to a life that happens
right now that is full of reality and allows us to see the
difference between what is and what is imagination. To
have an open mind and allow reality to be experienced is
the portal to total peace and freedom. How can I be so
sure about that? Because there is no suffering left in my
life, there is only the beauty of life itself that connects.
Connection happens through intuition, a form of real
connectedness that's beyond intellectual connection. It's
a connection with all bodies, minds and souls. It is the
sweetness of empathy and compassion that arises
through feeling what the intuition tries to express. The
intuition is nothing like a separate entity, it is all that is,
not more, not less. It is reality.

Intuition is our friend and the friend of everyone else and everything that is. Let me tell you a little and very simple daily story of mine. I travelled in a plane to Hong Kong and got super upset waiting for my food because they forgot to serve me and were not giving me attention when I asked about my meal. So from my point of view, this was the egoic identity that was fighting with what is. I wasn't listening to my intuition, just hearing my mind. If I went back in time and listened to my intuition, it would be empathic understanding, non-judgemental, and I would be in peace knowing I was actually not starving, I was just sitting there and would be pleased to get my food—a super-neutral thought.

Having the freedom to enjoy a beautiful movie on the plane or watch the sunset: they were the opportunities I had, and much more. I could maybe engage in a beautiful conversation with my neighbour instead of telling him how stupid everything was and getting angrier and angrier, so upset that I got a headache, believing my egoic identity that I was starving. Even if I just had a full bag of cedar nuts. So here is a beautiful example of listening to the intuition as a way of creating a healthy mind/body balance. After 10 minutes of waiting, my food arrived and I actually got an extra dessert because I was 'waiting'. If I would have believed reality and listened to my intuition I would have seen that they were just busy or maybe couldn't find my ordered food and still asked without making my body believe my imagination the mind. They were not ignoring me on purpose, they were doing the job they had to do: serve food and drinks during a specific time frame. So intuition shows us the truth that resides in reality and will always be presented in a warm-hearted way.

The following questions can help you to recognise intuition during your daily life when you are not experiencing peace, and they can be a portal to achieve the wisdom of intuition intellectually. Throughout the book you will find many different ways of utilising the mind as a tool to unpractise the practice of believing.

Let's start with the first introduction of the guide which is the 10 Point Intuition Cell-Awareness Method:

## Intuition Cell-Awareness Method

1. Do you have the feeling that something was or is strange, inconsistent or not right? Please describe it.

2. Write 1-3 advices from you to the person or moment on how it should be, act, behave or interact regarding to statement 1.

3.  Do you think that intuition guides you to a joyful life?

4.  Please describe the feelings and thoughts you have about the statement in question 1. How do you feel?

5.  Does the feeling of statement 1 bring you joy?

6.  Now go back to the moment of the statement from question 1. Do you think that your intuition was to let you receive the information from question 1. knowing that your intuition wants you to live in joy?

7.  What happens to you, how do you respond to yourself and/or your counterpart if you trust the statement from point 1?

8.  What would happen to your behaviour towards yourself, others and this particular moment if you were guided by your intuition?

9. In addition to the notes from 8, please specify exactly the moments in which the contrary statement took place or is taking place.

10. Now refer to statement 1. Use this as a mirroring practice. So relate it to you, contrary to others and contrary to the moment that you described. Then go to statement 2 and use it as a mirror for you and a mirror to the perspective of others, and find ways of turning it around.

Intuitive guidance practices will appear in different forms throughout this book; there will be similar questioning and reflecting exercises in different variations to school the mind for seeing and perceiving reality as it is and to perceive imagination from different angles.

I have learned that many of us confuse intuition with imagination. All those warnings, buzzers, concerns and worries are negative thoughts. They have the tendency to lead us away from what is really happening. They are not our intuition, they are imagination.

Colors blind the eye.
Sounds deafen the ear.
Flavors numb the taste.
Thoughts weaken the mind.
Desires wither the heart.

The Master observes the world
but trusts his inner vision.
He allows things to come and go.
His heart is open as the sky.

Lao Tzu.

*Tao Te Ching*, chapter 12
Translation by Stephen Mitchel

The egoic identity wants to fight with all that is. The egoic identity makes the mind travel to the past and to the future, to maybes and could-bes, becoming blind to what happens right in front of us. This vanishes the opportunity to listen to intuition.

The egoic identity loves to judge reality. And it is quite good at it. Most of the impressions we consume during the day are only a piece of reality, filtered by judgements and convictions. We consider it real; it feels real, but it is much more thought than reality.

Intuition is free of intellectualised judgement that closes us up. It shows us unfiltered reality. Only what we perceive with our two eyes, in this very moment, is reality. If we listen to our intuition, we can see what is real and what it is the thinking and believing mind wants us to consider real. Intuition questions all that creates suffering on this planet. It shows us what's behind the scenes. It is the realisation of peace and freedom in every human. Intuition is peace. Thus this is the mind that we use to feel the deep wisdom it has to offer; we may use it as a pointer to it. The process of deepening intuitive knowledge shall support to understand conceptually and integrate beliefs to understand what they are and then metabolise them effortlessly.

Intuition is letting the present moment sink in and all that comes with it. It is the opportunity to love the past and enjoy more deeply what is happening in this moment and what is real. The past can be a wonderful place to travel to, but too often we are looking back at things and we remember how we thought they were, instead of how they really were. Reality happens only in this moment and intuition shows us this wisdom.

Wisdom is a gift. If we clear all those assumptions and judgements, wisdom will lead us to freedom of mind. Without the judging mind, who would we be? We would be in love with all that is happening. Love would flood us. We would recognise what a loving and kind place our earth is.

Intuition always leads us to understand our and others' individuality. Intuition shows us how to be whole. All knowledge that this book offers to you is collected experience. It is achieved wisdom that is connected to scientific research or personal experiences to make it conceptual.

Let me ask you a question. Can you trust your intuition if it sends you on a road of suffering? A road built on judgements against others and ourselves? A road built on worries about past and future? A road built on resistance? Is that your intuition? You guessed it. It's not. It's imagination. If we find ourselves suffering, we have lost our intuition and the wisdom of love is hidden behind our thoughts and beliefs. Intuition will lift the weight that suffering carries and support us metabolizing with what we experience. The experience will not disappear it will be digested and if we open our hearts it is an offer to utilize it as a source of wisdom.

Allow me to elaborate on judgements. Judgements do not have to be evil. Many of them help us get through the day. However, all so often they filter reality without us realising. Our mind loves to label everything and judgements make great labels. I would love you to treat the mind as a friend. Learn how to be a lover of what is. Reality is always so much kinder than our convictions make us believe. Always!

If you take the path of intuition you will be welcomed in this life wherever you are. We all incarnate with an inner call even if you don't remember what was before this life. Intuition is not only a glimpse of true love. It is freedom and love itself. There is creation and potential from the view of intuition and there is destruction and non-potential so trust it will always guide you and remember that you are the perceiver of both. It will show you the source of existence. Nature is always evolving and there is no way to separate the way that you evolve and that nature evolves. The universe is constantly expanding; even if you don't live intuitively you will expand. If you understood that you may not need to read more. There is no way of not achieving a life that's led by intuition. It's our plan, a plan that was there before physical existence and we all compromise to it without a single compromise. When you expand your external world expands, when your external world expands your inner world expands.

What holds us back from living a life that's expanded in peace? Yes, you already know it: our traumas, beliefs and convictions. To access the same frequency that those traumas, beliefs and convictions have I invite you to use the creator part of it. Your intellect. It is an invitation for your intellect to see reality as it really is. Take your time and reflect and let this sink in where the external world makes you suffer. This is a wonderful tool where we can start to see reality if we come with an open heart and an open mind. It takes courage and truth, yes, it is being honest to one's self and becoming aware of the dream that imagination loves to sell to us. So how does it work to use the intellect? Take a deep breath, allow yourself to arrive before you go into it.

Have a look at you and all that is with kindness and curiosity.

If you have:

Anxiety at being alone, find where you choose to be alone.

Fear of not being loved, find where you don't love.

Anger at not being respected, find where you don't respect.

Upset because others treat you bad, find where you treat others bad.

Hate of people who hurt other people or entities, find where you hurt other people and entities.

# 3.    Experiencing Intuition

There is a huge gift we are all born with: a sound that tells us an intuitive truth. Often it is just covered behind our convictions. Our mind, our egoic identity and our imagination filter the sound. All you need is an open mind to lift those filters and experience reality as it is.

Let me tell you about an episode in my life when I was suffering. There had been a time when I had no access to my intuition, when my mind, my egoic identity and my imagination caused too much noise to hear the sound of truth. I actually was terrified, depressed, had anxiety attacks and I was super judgemental of myself and others.

Everything I consumed increased that terrifying experience. The news I read, the food I ate and the drugs I consumed all made me feel like I was living in hell. I was trapped in an ugly body, not knowing who I was, considering our earth the dirtiest, filthiest and deadliest place imaginable.

I wasn't kind to myself. I wasn't kind to my family. I was full of guilt. I was full of concepts of how life had to be, but how it never was. I was judging everything constantly because I couldn't experience my intuition. As long as I believed in my thoughts and concepts and not in my intuition, I was suffering. I often asked myself, 'How could I react that way? How could I do that to my family and friends? Why can't I stop it? Why am I so depressed? Why am I so angry? Why can't I live in peace while being alive?'

Today, I know I was trapped in a conviction. I thought there would be no other escape from suffering but leaving my physical body behind. When we believe what our mind, egoic identity and judgemental imagination tries to tell us, we will be suffering. If we live intuitively, we will live in love, freedom and peace of mind, wherever we are.

Intuition, as you start to listen to it, will become your best friend. It always wants you to be healthy, free and in peace. If there is no peace and freedom, it is the attempt of the egoic identity to fight with what is. The important thing to keep in mind is this: **If a belief or thought hurts, then it is not the intuition showing you reality.** Instead, it is the mind arguing with what is.

I came to see that this is true for every human being. This book starts by guiding you to listen to what your cells have to offer you, it is a guide to intuition. You can open it anywhere and with an open heart you will inspire your cells to speak louder to you. The practices will support in identifying what are beliefs and what is the intuition. Being led by the intuition means to arrive in reality, where the joy beyond peace, freedom and health is always present. Intuition for me is a vast experience with layers that are beyond a concept which would use intuition in a context only of having a good intuition when winning in the lottery, for example.

Again and again i come to realise that intuition shows us that life is our friend and the friend of everyone else and everything that is. Intuition is the opportunity to create an earth in peace full of empathy, compassion and love. It's for me, it's for you and it's for every living being on planet Earth. I'm looking forward with all of my heart to see you practise living intuitively.

To express yourself in freedom, you
must die to everything of yesterday.
From the 'old', you derive security;
from the 'new', you gain the flow

—Bruce Lee

# 4. Childhood Shaming and Intuition Trauma

Before I elaborate on the topic of how shaming cages the intuition and leads to social and ethical behaviour patterns, I want to tell you a little story of mine.

I went to class the first year of school and one day at the beginning of the year we had an exercise to learn to write one's favourite colour. The teacher asked me my favourite colour, and as always when I got this question I answered the rainbow colour.

He responded, That's not a colour, what is your favourite one?

I answered the colour rainbow.

He asked me again and said that I should not play games with him and say my favourite colour.

I said but it is the rainbow colour.

His response was, Leave the classroom now and wait outside till I call you again and leave the door open.

So I did and waited outside.

He asked all my other classmates.

And I heard colours from blue to green, rose, purple, black and white and then he called me in again.

He asked, Did you hear the answers of the others?

I responded, Yes I did.

With a commanding voice he said, SO, then you learned now on your own how to answer a question right. Please share your favourite colour with us, Patrick.

And I answered blue as he was wearing a blue shirt and hoped he would like this answer this time.

And indeed he said, Bravo, Patrick, let me show you how to write blue.


This is the Rainbow Cage.


Please be aware that the childhood shaming topic shall be read with an open heart and neutrality to understand rather than judge. Allow yourself to read with curiosity and be aware what intention you have while reading it.


Shaming in childhood is the main reason for alienation of intuition and fragmentation behaviour towards oneself and others which filters the intuitive love navigation. Shaming is on this planet like a social condition whose roots come from shaming and violent communication at the younger age. That leads to the constant public shaming of self and other and which is an increasingly popular epidemic that can damage and disturb our perception of self and others. It seems to be a rule not even to communicate shaming but hide the feeling of shame. If you don't know what I mean here with shame, let me explain. Shame is the mechanism that comes from evaluating one's self-image to an image of a considered better self or comparing to any other person that might conceptually have a value that's higher than mine. This will bring me to a self-experience where I don't see myself as worthy and trustful. What is the real reason for this going back to childhood? It is the social behaviour of needing to behave. This works like a sleeping pill for consciousness. This unconsciousness leads humans to social convictions and beliefs that shape the values in relations, it doesn't matter if they are values from different cultural backgrounds or social. I invite you here to reflect and don't drink the pill just uncritically to adopt social and cultural values.

What does shaming look like?

Degrading the perspectives and beliefs of others.

Judging for not being or acting the way we want someone to be.

Even shaming about conditions (illness is nothing to feel ashamed of).

When in communication we present ourselves superior to others.

It can be something even almost not recognisable like an eye roll when my friend or family member doesn't share the same values.

Showing and expressing that we are not giving value for the other's opinion that we disagree with or even condemn the opposite conclusion.

What happens if this takes place? I lose the beauty of life and can't see reality anymore, I only look at my convictions.

Okay, so let's say there is a dad that has a child, and his child wants to play with Dad's miniature cars that have an excellent value for him. Dad is telling the child yes, you can play with it but be a good boy, be careful that you don't play too wild, don't break it. While dad has been at work Mum is playing with your child, and the toy car and a wheel fall off. The child thinks for a minute and shows it to Mum, and the wise mummy says no problem, nothing lasts forever. So the child doesn't feel a lot about it and goes to play with his other friends. So then Dad comes home from the office and asks where the toy is and his wife tells him that it's in the living room, but the wheel broke. So Daddy goes to his child asking him why he didn't take more care. Telling him that he said it shouldn't be played with roughly, yelling at him for not taking responsibility, and for making his child more responsible he will take the money to repair it from his pocket money.

So here is the thing: first of all in this universe was at the beginning the word. That means whatever I pray for I get, even if it is just a warning instead of caring advice. So the mechanism that will be charging after this experience will be (if we would say it was a boy) that I wasn't a good boy shaming program and whenever the child does something that reminds him unconsciously about this experience the same mechanism will enter. Before the task or project and even in social life there will be a previous concern that it will not work the way it should so he should be over careful with things … overthinking and not being able to listen to the intuitive voice, what could metaphorically be the voice of the mum, is one of the things that take place. As soon as the inner guide should connect it will be immediately stoned with the pill of unconsciousness which filters the intuitive wisdom. So the copying that happens here is that whenever something isn't the way that social or cultural values want it to be we shape ourselves into a constant self-shaming machine, not listening anymore to the inner guide but to the idealistic identity. Be aware of your rainbow cages.

Shame is the emotion that mostly expresses its sensation from the belly to the head, and it is the result of demeaning values on how children should or shouldn't act. It's the result of idealisation instead of individualisation. This creates this feeling of being of less worth than others. This can be from feeling less intelligent, not that beautiful, less creative than others, not as sporty as our friends and classmates. Here once again, and this is essential to understand, the hidden principle shame is a cover up of the feeling of being less worthy than others. As soon as the children adapt to the values that are stamped onto them they receive a medal and as soon as they aren't meeting what those stamped values look like they are punished with shame. Socialised children crave for the conceptual benefits of love, respect, being a part of something, getting and giving, and protection from harm. So to get this sense of worth, believing that it might only be achieved through the pill of idealisation, shapes individuality into unconscious reactive formality.

As soon as children derive their sense of self from all that has been learned to do, inevitably the child gets into shame as soon as it doesn't fit with the values. As you probably all can sense, it's changing as now the earth and its new habitats are blooming with the light of consciousness that comes with individuality and spontaneous expression of self.

We have inherited a conceptual rather than an intuitive culture in which anger, violence, arrogance, competition and emotional degradation such as fear and hate are celebrated in the media and unexpressed when they would get the chance to flow from the instinctive behaviour rather than the mechanical stamped on. This mechanical stamped behaviour leads to a self-control mechanism that filters the intuitive wisdom which leads us to individuality.

Instead of inheriting the individuality that makes us really who we are, we are shaped only to inherit what is praised socially and culturally as excellent, because all that I inherited will feed me and I will use it to feed others. It will make me believe that it will save me from violence, will make me be loved and will meet my needs. Not matching the values of the stamp shows me how not to be loved, not to be seen and not to get my needs met. This fragmentation of the individual expression of self is the core mechanism to shame. Shame shapes the adapted self-image to prevent harm and the consequences that the taken behaviour would create. So any given moment the rules and values are not met or I would rather listen to my intuition than the conceptual values, I shame myself.

The duality mirror of shame is greatness, the hierarchical feeling of being superior or even better than others.

This egoic feeling of greatness works like the addiction to the pill of dumped consciousness. We create a mask, hiding our essence behind this identity of being great, and as soon as the identity gets the chance, it gets easily tempted to shaming others. Whenever we do that we as well shame our cells. This covers not only reality it covers our cells. The word shame roots from the old

English 'hama' which simply means 'covering'.
Covering all cells within the body with shame. It is for
me like glueing as well. Glueing the past on my cells and
covering them with an experience that then blocks my
natural receptivity to nutrients. Being in shame is
making my cells feel bad. It is inferiority shown to any
entity. Showing them how inferior they are which leads
to an even more significant hierarchical gap. The usual
practice of this mechanism is the conceptual, cultural
otherwise called ethical shaming, making the other sense
to be less moral, noble, ethical or less smart, which too
often happens as we believe the labelling thoughts of the
mind. Usually it is correlated to a situation where the
identity wants to override the other's individual
experience. Wishing to convince that its own knowledge
or perspective is a part of its being and that the person
itself is wrong rather than the view and that now their
perspective should be adopted and taken as a part of who
the person is. The primary goal of cultural, ethical
shaming is to prove one's perspective as 'right' and the
other one's as 'wrong'; rather than to have an open heart
listen to the natural intuitive voice and use the mind
instead of shooting the shaming weapon to open a space
for embracing different perspectives.


The cultural, ethical shaming is an egoic self-destruction
mechanism which results from the rainbow cage that I
love to call the Trojan horse identity that's hidden
through well-articulated arguments and reasoning. As
soon as this fantastic shaming method gets fusion with
the self-righteousness, the outcome will be the cage of

an intellectually valued life experience that's stamped just for idealisation rather than an experience that the individual leads through oneness and intuition. The fusion of shaming and self-righteousness is a mechanism that devalues not only individuality and damages the stream that nourishes us with intuitive behaviour, it hurts our genes, cells and therefore our physiological body. Those shaming traumas can be even taken over from past lives or genetically given from the parents. An intention that rises from peace or curiosity's open space to understand the difference between what just has been not the way it could have been instead of identifying and adding the shaming mechanism to the self-image as being 'wrong' and 'unethical' or I am right and ethical, instead of utilising the experience as something to learn from than take it as a part of the identity. We are our stories, but we are as well much more than that. We are the source of existence, and we are life itself.

The feeling of shame is an underlying root cause for every disorder involved with inflammation, where the immune system shuts down or even attacks the body itself. Mostly when a person experiences shame the first reaction would be to fight any symptoms or expressions that would be shown. As it is not felt and experienced with an open heart, it starts to inherit in the physiology. If shame is pushed away and fought against it is like fighting against oneself. Therefore then it is the person itself attacking the personal natural way of expressing it and caging it inside the body. If the energy that's released from shame is being fought back or held from oneself and not shown, it causes a fight against oneself.

The feeling of shame is a mechanism where the body uses the energy of stored traumata that can even be older than what we remember. Besides very traumatic moments it happens especially where the social and ethical values have been taken over, have been 'downloaded'. Shame works hand in hand with the egoic (which is always the romantic as well) motivation to change the self because of doctrines, values and beliefs. We are grown up to love a drama. Having someone around you with the shaming mechanism can be recognised by a constant state of defending oneself and defending the identity of others, blaming experiences from the past, blaming others and projecting on them the same they are doing but cannot consciously see yet.

It's a constant attempt to show where the others are wrong, to absorb the energetic attention that's received through victimisation where the person even can get very aggressive and choleric or flegmatic as well if the self-image needs aren't met. The egoic self-image grows in an unlimited amount that it almost can consume and take over the whole experience. People with these shaming mechanisms believe that it is indeed needed to devalue, shame and even violate another as long as one's needs and vampirism of moral righteousness are matched. It's a constant self-evaluation of showing and perceiving only oneself's parts that are considered

39

reasonable and shame away what isn't nice in the view
of the personal values.


Please invite yourself here to understand that any person
who suffers from the shaming mechanism is looking for
a conceptual way of self-love by seeking it in others and
that's very far away from loving oneself. This
mechanism continually finds reasons why one's life isn't
the way it should be and therefore as soon as the
experience is the way it wanted to be finding a reason to
again see life as lacking and creating even a larger self-
righteousness image. I invite you here to consider that
shame is the best reminder to connect to oneself, to
invite not beliefs or convictions but to invite yourself to
yourself. For me, guilt is not the call to change into
social or ethical behaviour, it is my body making me
aware that I'm not acting out of my soul values.


So how do I get out of shaming or support someone who
has a shaming mechanism and is asking for support?


First of all, it is essential to recognise the moment that
shame appears and instead of identifying with it and
trying to fight it, invite it to be wholly experienced. Get
aware of the same mechanism and write it down or
express it in words. But rather than saying and
identifying the 'I' with 'I am shamed' allow yourself to
see it as an experience which could sound like I'm
experiencing shame. Why is that difference significant?

As soon as I allow myself to integrate whatever comes, I become whole, and I allow myself to evolve, let things pass and see that all exactly happens only once. Shame isn't different here. My choice here is, I just don't believe the bla bla bla machine in my head anymore, I do my best to rather see reality. When the machine starts talking too much and I'm in the mood for a little romanticism then I just start rolling my eyes, and show the mind it is not the only one who can moan a little. It's like making a little party with all selves in the mind.

That's a technique that always works to make life more or less dramatic whatever the intention is. Sometimes fighting fire with fire can ease and release space for new. Finding the harmony between my needy dramatism and my fulfilled parts is like baking the perfect cake. It is like hacking one's inner beliefs and self-conversation mechanisms. It's a very sharp balance to not shame inner parts of oneself but yes, integrate and play with them. All those parts have their individuality and as well the capacity to understand what we want to communicate.

It is important for me to keep in mind that in the beginning was the word. As soon as a person starts to devalue, shame, bully, fight or violate another's space that's when the person told the universe what it should deliver because it knows what is expected. My beliefs on the world and others shape without exception the experience of being human.

Take the first moment you recall where you felt
ashamed, this can be from a moment where you felt
down or dropped an item to something where it was that
you have felt ashamed by a stranger, family member or
friend.


Feel the moment, imagine with your mind as exact as
you can the moment.

How did you feel?

How do you think that the others around you felt?

Do you think you would feel ashamed if no one was
there?


Now taking the perspective of the persons around you.
Try to take on their shoes.


How did it make them feel?

What did they from their individual experience noticed?

Was there something the persons around you judged?

Was there something you judged?

Now allow yourself to integrate this experience. Feel it
from both perspectives. Allow yourself to metabolise
and transform it into a source of wisdom.


From now on may I recognise when I feel ashamed.
When I'm shaming and turn it into interaction rather

than reaction. May I follow the voice of my inner wise guidance to reside within me and allow others to reside within them the way they are.

We can reduce the shaming mechanism to one another if we, before we speak or after a moment where we weren't agreeing with someone wanting to be righteous too, take a moment's reflection of stillness, be present and ask ourselves, 'At this very moment, am I or was I connected?'

Am I connected to my intuition right now? Intuition always leads to peace, so here I can take short moments to reflect if the answers to the following question give peace or a feeling of righteousness.

What will my actions or words make me and the other feel?

How would I feel and how would I react if someone said or responded this way to me?

When is it that I'm expressing myself the same way that the person in front of me is?

Every shamer or person that's shamed cares actually very much about the cause and the impact of what they are doing. Often we forget that this person that is shaming us or we are shaming is a human like us, with personal needs, struggles, feelings, wishes, and that every word that is spoken will have an impact on the next moment.

So what other than ethical or social can impact the expression of intuition? Let's say you would be born into a religious group, it happens too often that we just adopt the convictions of this specific group. So rather than inviting ourselves and the inner guide we choose unconsciously to be idealistic rather than consciously intuitive. If the moment's reflection of stillness gives you not the total picture, I invite you to reflect deeper as soon as you experience shame or are shaming someone else to take the 10 Point Intuition Cell-Awareness Method for reflection on intuition. Why intuition, what has it to do with shame? The process will support you in identifying convictions, seeing when it is that you can be a mirror to yourself and getting inspiration to live from your intuitive wisdom. Intuition is free of judgement. It shows us our unfiltered reality. It shows us how to perceive and unpractise our beliefs on being wrong or being right and find the space beyond being right and wrong. If we heed our intuition, we can see what is truly real. Intuition helps us differentiate what originates from our soul's plan or what the believing mind, traumas and convictions want us to consider to be the reality. Living from our intuition is the way to metabolise what has been in the past and disidentify from it as if it would be me and integrate it as an experience. Intuition shows us what lies behind the scenes. It is the realisation of peace and freedom in everyone. Intuition is peace.

Being wise is finding a middle way between emotional mind and rational mind. Having a wise mind

— Dr Zumra Atalay.

# 5.  Trauma and Emotional Responses

Trauma itself creates even after the experience physiological responses within the body which we often then call emotions. So what is an emotion? An emotion works like an in-the-body-sensed experience which is created through a stimuli in our cells which can occur spontaneously, subconsciously, through sensory organs and thought patterns which then is translated through the brain and physiologically experienced. Emotions can be experienced in an extreme variety. What happens in a trauma-stored emotional response is that the body activates emotionally and through physiologically felt experiences from stimuli in the external world which are believed to be threatening. Those responses as well occur in settings which could be beneficial rather than threatening. Which can go from hearing the keychain in front of the door when a loved one is coming home to a smell of something burning in the kitchen.

Emotions constantly interact with the way that we experience what we think that reality is. They are a great source to remind us to review if the emotions are connected to the present reality or the imaginary reality created by the beautiful and dramatic mind. The mind is the best and most dramatic regisseur that you can imagine. He loves it tasty and eccentric. The best movies are experienced in the imagination; they are so real that often we think that what we feel is reality and it's always without exception just filtered reality. Seeing the opportunity that all emotions can be a way of experiencing life with more tastes, a little more extravagant and dramatic, leaves in me the feeling of being on a big, exciting playground where my curiosity allows me to look beyond my beliefs.

We are most nearly ourselves when we
achieve the seriousness of the child
at play

—Heraclitus

# 6. Medusa Mechanism

The thing about trauma is that if we do not learn to integrate it we disassociate from it and create a segregation from the identity and intuition. It's a split of wholeness. So in this segregation humans start to identify in different moments with one specific type of personality, thinking that they have only one part in which cages them to act like in a roleplay. What actually happens is that in the inside and in the external world there manifest different identities that are not seen as integrated because it doesn't fit social and ethical behaviour. It's like a trap full of traps which I love to call the Medusa mechanism. So what is the Medusa mechanism? It is the technique that brings humans after a trauma in the fragmented self-image where they see themselves as not enough or too much for oneself and others. Like an analogy, each snake on the head of Medusa is a fragmentation that immediately turns into the direction of any soul that is around. Each snake represents a fragmented part of oneself and as a symptom of it the snake starts to label the other as being better, worse, or unacceptable the way that the counterpart is.

In a holistic living person all sense organs are the portal to live intuitively and live whole. For this analogy I will use the eyes that can perceive the light of every existing entity.

In the Medusa mechanism the eyes that should perceive reality, soul, light and dark are not able to see those. It works like a protective shield of the split identity. As soon as one fragmented piece, which here would be a head of a snake, is looking into the direction of reality, soul, light and dark as one and would perceive an opportunity to see oneself no more as separated it turns the other into stone. It happens immediately as the eyes meet the eyes of the other. As the eyes are the portal of the soul the identity blocks it. This perspective of the Medusa mechanism is a self-protection mechanism which roots are found in childhood shaming. Medusa is known for being very terrifying and ugy that if any men even look at her eyes, they would immediately be turned into stone. In the story Perseus was able to not turn into stone by looking at her reflection in a mirror. Even though he was technically looking at her, just with a mirror, he did not turn into stone. If we invite ourselves to look at every person from the third perspective, here is the mirror that is the portal to integrate duality.

So how to integrate the Medusa mechanism so that the soul is recognised again? I want to invite you to sit still.

Take a breath, arrive within yourself and read with an open heart. Reflect on any situation that might arise reading this.

Let's practise to unpractice. Go deep. Use your imagination.

I started to criticise someone...

(take a moment and reflect when was the last time)

I holify and glorify another person when...

(take a moment and reflect when was the last time)

Now reflecting on both moments—it can be something you consider as not that important such as a criticism of another's haircut, shoes or something like the person is dishonest or unfriendly. Write down what it is that you degraded about somebody, describing in three words what it was that disturbed you about the other. Dig into your wounds.

For example:

The person is not caring, a terrible dresser, not intelligent enough, is aggressive... Now reflecting on both moments, write down what it is that you degraded about yourself while glorifying the other, describing in three words what comes up for you... After that put the three words in a sentence. It could be :

The person is not caring, dresses terribly, is aggressive.

Now I have to invite myself into myself, look at me with the mirror to not turn myself or others into stone. For that I need to see where it is in my life that I am not caring, dress terribly, am aggressive.

Sit still with that for a moment.

After that put three words that wound you in a row. Words which could be the opposite to you of when you glorify someone. For example:

This person is pretty, so inspiring and everyone loves this person.

Which could be turned into:

I 'm ugly, useless, unloved. Reflect and look where that is taking place.

Now I have to invite myself into myself, look at me with the mirror to not turn myself or others into stone. For that I need to see where it is in my life that I am not ugly, useless, unloved.


This is a practice to exercise the mirroring of the Medusa mechanism instead of cutting off the head. You can do as many turnarounds as you want, not only to yourself but as well to others. This is the practice to live intuitively, it is a practice to unpractice the convictions and beliefs that came from childhood trauma through ethical and social values and guidelines.


Like Byron Katie said, 'Placing the blame or judgment on someone else leaves you powerless to change your experience; taking responsibility for your beliefs and judgments gives you the power to change them.'

If you allow yourself to look at it but now utilise the mirror and see what is a reflection and what is projection then you will perceive the other without turning anyone into stone or being turned into stone. You will metabolise what is stored within your cells. The only way to live whole is to 'know thyself' as inscribed in the pronaos of the Temple of Apollo at Delphi. To know yourself is to understand one's inner world and external world. It can't be understood by the cutting of the head and therefore think the Medusa mechanism will be gone or just letting the Medusa mechanism head take over. One must integrate both. Take this as a daily practice to take home any fragmentation.

Turn your wounds into wisdom

—Oprah Winfrey

# 7. What Is Intuition Telling Me About Suffering?

It seems that suffering is what we all have to go through whether we want to or not, if it is needed or not, if it is wished or not. I want you to listen to my words with lots of attention now. Suffering that's experienced without awareness of the cause is like a flu that's very persistent in coming and going. But it shouldn't be seen as a condition, more like something where order is calling to be placed again. Suffering is the call to connect again to an intuitive way of living.

I want to underline the importance and background of this gift of living intuitively. Intuition can just happen but whenever we suffer it is hidden behind what we may not be able to perceive. Remember to strengthen intuition there are tools that utilise the beautiful mind. It is a general combination of self-reflection, practical tools of unpractising beliefs, individual questioning and ongoing self-liberation to help develop intuitive wisdom which is a tool to thrive in our individuality. All that you find written here shall be a support to presence deepening and giving insights and pragmatic approaches to combine what personal experience and science delivers to live a holistic, intuitive and integrated life.

If I would get dramatic I could say that the mental disorder spread on this planet more than anything else is the condition to make oneself believe, filtering one's inner intuitive wisdom. What does that mean, to make oneself believe? If you have a look at the state of current consciousness it is evolving to a state of realising that there is only oneness. Looking at the way social and ethical values are stamped onto us it is easy to understand why we rather live idealistically than intuitively. Those values make us constantly think about ourselves, having self-conversations in the mind, reliving moments and imagining moments that have not even arrived.

Let me tell you something here: the mind and all that he is showing us can be the most beautiful way to create and as well the most wonderful way to destruct. It is my choice what I listen to, if I listen to the constant speaking voice or the silence behind the words and the flow evolution that happens listening to intuition. Here I'm speaking about a behaviour that's not harmonious. In this universal dimension everything is in constant creation and transformation, destruction exists in the one that believes in it. Life itself is occurring transformation.

I can be the one to choose the transformation of consciousness or just follow the subconscious beliefs. The mind is running all the time and it seems that it is already exhausted but it looks like there is no way out of this constant rushing. It's like a repeating long disc that never stops. This noise is hiding the inner wisdom that intuition has to offer. Most beliefs and convictions are created in childhood and we really don't need them but it seems like they need us to survive. Many of those filtering-mind-created beliefs don't have any other tasks but to prove oneself constantly right or wrong. To turn into doubts which always correlate to fear.

Doubt is a call of love to readjust the inner compass. Feeling doubt allows you to see that it was too often when you haven't been within yourself but seeking yourself outside. This stream of self uninvite is the root of any disturbances that lead to an unpleasant human experience. It could be said that most of the population are not believing in themselves which is in essence therefore the mind creating a belief that believes in oneself. And, my beloved friends, I want to tell you that if you invite silence into your mind with the same quality as if it were your best friend, that is integration.

It seems to be a chronic condition to have the beauty of reality filtered through convictions. But here I tell you from all of my heart it is not! We are given the opportunity to look beyond. To use the power that we have within us not only to heal our emotional selves but be an inspiration for every person that interacts with us. This happens when you let the light of intuition shine through you. It will not only be you who recognises this light, everyone around you will be an inspiration for you, and you for others. Living intuitively is beyond any concepts. I use the mind here as the program to download this trainable ability. It is the mind that makes us practise all those beliefs and it is the mind that makes us unpractice them to come to the space that's beyond all intellect and within all that's intellectual.

So I wish that you can open your heart to all these blessings, and let them flow through you. Then everyone whom you will meet on this day will be blessed by you. Just by your eyes, by your smile, by your touch. Just by your presence. Let the gratefulness overflow into blessing all around you. And then, it will really be, a good day

—Brother David Steindl-Rast

# The condition to make oneself believe

**The condition to make oneself believe** is a belief system where one is convinced that any external or internal condition is the root of a life that is not lived in joy. It is the mechanism that drives the identity into a pattern where there can always be found a reason why emotional healing can't take place. It could be parents that were unable to love, a family driving one crazy, colleagues in school, university or work, material wealth or the lack of a life that is considered comfortable. As soon as I do not integrate those chapters of my life and use them to shame and victimise myself or others there is no healing happening. Emotional health is created through the portal of intuition which allows me to see reality and reality is the integration of everything that was and will be to come together with the only thing that really exists. The only thing that exists as the power of healing is the integration of all of this, and then I open my eyes and look around and see myself and all that I perceive with these two eyes as reality.

Here is a practice. Take a moment and reflect on a situation that is coming into your mind now which disturbed you, made you angry or made you deeply suffer.

Imagine the moment and write down what advice you would give to the persons that are in this moment or how the situation itself should have been.

The advice could look like this:

My parents should be more kind, loving and caring whenever they speak to me.

Now take a moment and read it.

Please be honest in the maximum amount that your awareness allows you to be. See where it is that you could take those advices that you just gave to yourself. For every piece of advice find at least one situation where you should have been following the advice.

This is an honest exercise where you need to invite yourself to yourself. Allow yourself to practise your beliefs about what you think you have experienced and mirror it to yourself.

Now take another moment and close your eyes; take a few deep breaths and come back to your answers.

Write the answers you have written as a direct order to yourself, which could look like: I will be more kind, loving and caring to my family whenever I speak. Ask yourself if you can do this. Feel your body's pendulum and see if you can do this. I will be more kind, loving and caring to my family whenever I speak. Your answer should be just a yes or no and the answer will determine if you will be kind, loving and caring or if not.

If your answer was yes, for the upcoming weeks every time before you speak to the person that was making you feel not cared and loved, take a moment to invite yourself into yourself and for this practice have an open heart and speak: 'The person in front of me wants the same, to be treated in a kind, loving and caring manner; therefore, I will be more kind, loving and caring in any given moment that I speak to them.'

If your answer was no, redo the exercise in a moment where you feel you can have an open heart and proceed in the upcoming weeks the same as described and use the magical words before every conversation.

This is the recipe of life
said my mother
as she held me in her arms as I wept
think of those flowers you plant
in the garden each year
they will teach you
that people too
must wilt
fall
root
rise
in order to bloom

—Rupi Kaur

# 8. Intuitive Activation of Healing Processes

Here I would love to elaborate on the most powerful tool of self-healing that exists. Intuitive medicine. Which for me is the combination of scientific studies with the felt intuitive experience for best healing support. Individual health and vitality is understood and achieved through a clear vision. Through the ability of seeing reality. The tool that I would love to give you is intuitive healing with the power of the mind. Everybody has this strength to self-heal, every entity on this planet has the potential to intensify self-healing. The gift to heal is something that naturally occurs in every organism. Whenever your body gets damaged or sick it tries its best to heal itself. Whenever you hurt your skin, bones or organs your body heals itself. After a period the damages that occurred are healed.

After a surgery, for example, it's the physician helping you to heal, he isn't healing you. It's your body that's healing itself. You don't need to tell your body consciously to heal. It just happens. Cells know exactly what they have to do. They have inherited the building plan on how to heal to benefit the reproduction of the physiological structure that we call body. But here we know from research that it is the power of the mind or what we call placebo that can strengthen the healing. If you are aware of this you enable yourself to activate this super power of strengthening the process of self-healing. In the beginning was the word. So here I want to invite you with an open heart to first integrate all that you might be pushing away of being sick and invite it. Welcome it with an open heart and then allow yourself to release what you believe about what is illness and what is health. With this you use your creation powers. Healing is just a tool to lead attention to a spot where healing should take place. Intention of healing is here crucial.


Negative self- identification with a condition leads to vaster degeneration of our cellular health. So if I lost myself in identification with a condition I can use the intuitive healing method with self-created convictions.

# 9. Practise to Intensify Self-Healing

Take a paper and pen and answer following questions. The answer shall be only in three examples per question.

For example:

Where is it that I'm not whole?

Name … (Work/ college), Name …(Family), Name... (Partner)

You might see that things can be repetitive or totally different; that is all fine. We are all individual and everybody experiences things differently.

So start with answering following questions:

Where is it that I'm not whole?

Where is it that I'm not happy?

Where is it that I'm not giving love in my life?

Where is it that I'm not connected to myself and others?

Where is it that I'm not healthy and feeling the vitality my body has to offer?

Now please answer in the same way for the following questions. Here answers can be per question examples in sentences or note.

Where is it that I'm not letting somebody else be whole?

Where is it that I'm not letting somebody else be happy?

Where is it that I'm not giving love in my life to somebody else or me?

Where is it that I don't want to be connected to myself and others?

Where is it that I'm not allowing or accepting others to be healthy and vital in situations that I think aren't healthy?

Now allow yourself to invite yourself back to yourself. Let the past imagination go. And center your energy in the presence. Arrive within your cells.

Take the moments that you recognised where you did not allow the other to be healthy and wish them well. May you be in health, love, freedom and peace.

Then wish yourself well. May I be in health, love, freedom and peace.

*I realised my mind is my medicine.*

All in this universe works like a mirror, all that I give is what I receive. Getting aware of it allows me to integrate my whole being and not only the things I conceptually want to see.

The answers that you got from these questions is such a precious wisdom that will help you to apply health not only for yourself but yes, to see that healing is a collaborative experience.

Identification of the human mind with a condition of others or the condition of oneself works like a spell holding yourself back from healing and not allowing the other to heal. That happens not consciously. It's like a mechanism which can be even rooted in trauma of early age. Only the integration of intuition which is the realisation of oneness and wholeness is the tool for healing. When I allow myself to see every person whole as they are with or without a condition I give them space to evolve. If I don't I curse them and myself to not be able to heal. How free the individual frequency of the whole being is expressed.

People that allow themselves to unbelieve what they are believing about others create such a clear light that they heal without words. The body on this dimension may decay but to be in existence and heal in existence is beyond time and space structures. With an open heart I invite you once again to trust the wisdom of your intuition, there is nothing to shame or be ashamed of while having a condition not considered healthy. When the mind turns still and presences arise within all cells we might feel things in the body we couldn't sense before. When this is happening this is your invitation from your body to get into the just mentioned practice to intensify self-healing. When silence arises the body speaks to you. Shows what health means to your individuality and where it is that the body can't metabolise what has been experienced. This can be an experience of physiological digestions like foods, drinks, environmental factors, cosmetica and other substances. It can be as well psychological moments, past experiences, thoughts, happenings, old trauma that hasn't been metabolised. Intuition will lead you to understand and get gifted with the freedom that it has to offer.

Belief is when a person thinks something to be the way they think it is with or without there being any proven evidence. Another way of defining belief can be a mental representation of a self-image to make sure that something is true. Beliefs originate from all that we ingest, what we hear, see and experience, what we keep on hearing and seeing from the external world ever since we were children and as well even before that! Those beliefs are shaped by one or several experiences which shape the individual expression of self. The beliefs I'm elaborating on here are the ones that do not originate from empirical evidence.

Beliefs can get so strong that they even interact with not only soft but strong physiological behaviour changes. What does that mean exactly? Social experience, diet and nutrition, and exposure to toxins interact with behavioural epigenetics where the expression of genes is influenced by experiences and the environment. This as well shapes each habitant's individual expression here on Earth. And it's all interconnected with our personal behaviour, cognition, personality and the way we experience mental health.

A 'belief' in which an identification with personal attitudes towards oneself and others is within true or false convictions and concepts is the Trojan horse that can hold us from experiencing the intuitive wisdom that is beyond the physiological expression. A belief requires a behaviour in which no awareness of the subconscious and conscious parts of oneself, others or the whole is experienced. The reaction on my belief is what shapes my world and how beautifully dramatic I decorate it. Let me give you an practical and very simple example: let's say that the weather prognosis for tomorrow is sunny and I plan a nice trip and the next morning I wake up and it's all cloudy and rainy. If I believe that it should have been sunny and that that's the reason I can't take my trip or the trip can't give me amazement then I'm not aware that it isn't the weather that's the reason I can't take the trip. My expectation is that a nice trip is dependent on the way the weather is and which even can go so far that there will be not be an alternative as a result of the stress that was experienced when a belief was not fulfilled. On the opposite side, if a belief is fulfilled it shows how great one can manage the individual emotional expression when the sun is shining, only until you lose your cellphone on the hike... And there it is again, where the awareness of the subconscious and conscious parts of oneself, others or the whole experience is the way to listen to intuition; it's the light that shows what's beyond beliefs and invites every so-called good or bad experience.

Between stimulus and response there is a space.
In that space is our power to choose our
response. In our response lies our growth and
our freedom

—Viktor E. Frankl Austrian Neurologist

Just to bring a little abstraction to the topic of beliefs, if asked 'Do you believe that crocodiles wear sunscreen? How do you feel thinking about a crocodile using sunscreen? Can you believe a crocodile would wear sunscreen?' you know guessing is just fun and maybe your answer is yes or no despite the fact that you may never have seen, thought or talked about this before.

Beliefs and the way we act can be shaped by what we perceive in childhood, for example on soaps, movies, Hollywood, social rules, advertising form the personal beliefs, just by repeating something over and over again or having several moments where we experience emotional traumas associated with a similar situations, showing the way sexuality should look like and even how the act of sex should be, what beauty looks like or anything else that creates a strong emotional experience and sense of self.

When we are born we rise with an individual and intuitive wisdom which integrates the identity. It's an integration of the given self with its personal expression. As soon as there is a segregation of one part of oneself which is ethical or socially not approved in this moment, the perception of the mirror of self-reflection starts to break in parts. The egoic filter mechanism is created. It is this egoic filter mechanism that clouds the wisdom of intuition.

Let me tell you here that to see an image of oneself or others as soon as their name appears is normal. And I want to encourage you and invite you with all of my heart to allow yourself to see the image that arises without any labelling. What I mean with that is letting the image arrive, notice the story that may come with it and take the freedom of letting the image in the mind be and do whatever it wants to recognising that this is imagination. Allow your attention and consciousness to flow through this imagination and as soon as you shall see the person allow the person to be the person that you are seeing in front of you with your two eyes. Allow yourself to see the person without remembering anything you have ever experienced or think you will experience with that person. This is when you are connected to soul, to the essence, to the source of existence, integrating reality. Your eyes are the portal to the soul and the mind is the beautiful tool to make life more romantic or dramatic which can be a lovely experience when it is lived with awareness of the subconscious and conscious belief patterns. Only when I unpractice believing I return my natural given gift of instinctive intuition which always wants the best for me. Normally when you have the image of I or others it happens in 'the eye of imagination' so the way that 'the mind is seeing the I or others.'


You are here (reading, listening) to dig deeper and find out how to reach the full potential of intuition. This happens when I give room. I have a sense of the other when I'm believing what I think I know about the person or the object. I see the reality of me and the other when I'm still.

Coming again to see what intuition is, it can show me that there does not exist problems in this world for me. There are only different ways. Living intuitively gives me the freedom to choose to believe my thoughts or to use the curious and peace-giving experience of my inner wisdom.

Only inviting myself to myself gives me the effortless power to do what my soul's plan is. When I arrive within me I bring myself with all my cells alive. There is an intelligence that's beyond what we could even try to manage with our mind. It's everywhere in the body. It is led through the principle of universal creation which has in it the building plan of the physiological behaviour, for example, how our body has to self-organise itself as well. It is the guide that regulates and controls the way that the 3-D physiology acts here on Earth. It's so beautifully made that we do not need to take care with our mind of all those biochemical processes, as the body, as it is in a holistic state, tells us all it needs instinctively.

Every cell, every molecule, every atom and all that's beyond has its intuitive wisdom on how to act to be able to interact. It has an state of stillness and intention which then creates reaction. This applies mostly to the physiological manifestations, where matter underlays laws, which for me all refers to the extension from the second till the third dimensional space. If we would use a model of the physical universe which has no time as value but in which all known manifestations of matter exists we give it freedom to be whatever it wants to. In higher dimensions the laws may work differently. That's often a reason as well why after a fresh incarnation people get so frustrated when they don't remember that they are not separated physiological matter.

The mind as well is wonderful in creating stories on how to feel separated as it can be often dramatic to be separated from the sense of being connected while having a physical body. Just imagine yourself if you would enjoy conversation and maybe have daily contact with your family and best friends and are feeling that sense of social connection. Then you decide to do a new project and go to an island, bringing your phone to be sure to talk daily to them and there is no Wi-Fi, no internet, no telephone... and to make it more dramatic you even forget about all that happened before you came to the island. You will feel in your heart that there is something, something you shall remember. For some people it can be relieving, for some traumatic, but in the end what matters is that we invite ourselves to the island and then create out of the inner wisdom the project that we came to do. We are social beings and we thrive on spiritual and physiological connection. Without those two, as humans here at this 3-D universe there is no possibility to reproduce, to create, to live.

Everybody has the wisdom on how to behave to be able to express themselves. Here is just a little thought about it. Expression of the body can be in degeneration and regeneration. So each body has a puzzle which consists of metaphysical and physical. Each physical has a metaphysical and learning how to fit the piece on the other helps to decode the individual patterns that each body has. So by decoding not only the functionality how your individual body works on a normal daily basis but as well understanding how to reorganise and metabolise transgenerational trauma, trauma of this life and past life periods, is here essential. It is like finishing the puzzle to see the whole plan and the funny thing is that the puzzle is a fractal. You will experience that it can be finished and as it is finished you recognise it will never be finished.

Please be aware that as soon as you should use your individuality as a tool to criticise yourself, others, make yourself less, victimise yourself and others, that this may be a Trojan horse thought pattern.

Source individuality for me is what distinguishes me from others without making myself better or worse than others. The source individuality, which is connected to intuition, is the effortless reorganisation or rearrangement of my biological system in its best way it can. It is taking notice which patterns come out of my soul plan, individual biological expression, and which are compulsive and impulsive behaviour from stamped-on beliefs that we get from social or ethical values. Living intuitively allows me to see those patterns and identify them to reconnect to my inner guide. Learning about the self, connecting to the cellular wisdom having 'cellf-awareness'.

Self-awareness is the capacity for introspection and the ability to recognise oneself as an individual separate from the environment and other individuals.... While consciousness is being aware of one's environment and body and lifestyle, self-awareness is the recognition of that awareness

—Self-awareness: Wikipedia

We are never in the same mood, feeling or acting the same way. Sometimes nature sends us bad weather for a couple of days and sometimes the sun is there all the time. But if it is very dry because of too much sun and rain is coming plants become happy, if there is too much rain they may die. If then the sun comes after too much rain they become happy but then if the sun is there too long they dry out their happiness. And even after all that they will never stop to evolve and to keep doing what they are meant to do.

# 10.  Starting to Develop Intuition

The quality of our presence in this given moment changes our experience as a human. Why does intuition matter? In the busy, modern world intuition leads to general wellbeing.

How do we begin to develop intuition better? By recognising thoughts that make us feel bad, thoughts that make us feel good, thoughts that bring us to a judgemental behaviour or experience any kind of suffering. If there is war in the mind, intuition is calling you to experience peace. When we are connected to intuition we are being present.

As we are more present in this given moment, we improve the sensibility of what is happening in our mind, what is happening in reality and how our body responds to it.

We all can live intuitively in any moment. There are several ways to use the conceptual mind to practise and enter a life in peace and freedom, like meditation or questioning beliefs and convictions.

This whole experience lit a big fire within me to better understand not only the spirituality of humans but as well the physiology and how it shapes our experience. My inspiration guides me often not only into old wisdoms but yes, into modern science which gave me new insights to understand what I had wonderfully experienced and how to give it further, how to share it with the world. Through intuition we create a state, or it can be called a practice of 'cellfulness', inviting oneself into one's cells. Intuition creates awareness that what we let inside our body might interact with physiological responses and trigger thought patterns. I started communicating with my cells.

In this book are acceptance, contemplative, and Emotional self-expression practices to arrive in the present moment and connect to the cellular wisdom to better understand how to metabolise the past and how to open the cells to the kindness of reality for a wisely chosen future. It will have practical applications of mental and physiological cleansing that I use. It supports in integrating convictions and distractions of the egoic identity that always want to fight with the present moment.

Intuition is the gateway to free the mind and the world from all apparent suffering.

# 11. Mirror of Unacceptance

Here allow yourself to seek the direct experience, applying knowledge can be practical thus be aware my intention is not to give you something to believe, copying and be repeating. Rather just see it as a momentum when you experience this book. It's a call for a conceptual practice but for one that shows what's hidden beyond the understanding of individuality. Yes, it is to express your individual intuitive self with all that you have learned.

It doesn't matter where you are coming from, what you have studied, which movies, books, poets or artists inspire you. It doesn't matter what university you attended or what kind of certificate or degree you achieved. It is about your inner wisdom.

Curiosity and an open heart will engage with the opportunity to get inspired from all that is and evolve in a more holistic and healthier approach. What I want you to experience is yourself.

As you read here you will recognise that you know much more about this topic than you could even imagine. Wisdom is within all of us. You may think this book or any other source will give you more wisdom, thus the real wisdom of live is stored within you it is a matter of unlocking and understanding it. What it may give you is other perspectives. You will recognise that some very deep topics may arise and give you the opportunity to get inspired from them. All that's written here is just a reminder that all we experience is a mirror to what we think is reality. Intuition is the call to be the mirror. It's travelling into yourself to an inner journey and from there to look into the external world and the other way around. Your life is a constant growing book where you can draw the most amazing knowledge from. This is related to every aspect of life. To unpractise all that filters the only thing you need to do is be open-hearted, open-minded and be honest to yourself. The biggest judge is the own mind. It too often shows us life and wants us to believe what we think about it is true but actually, it is filtered by our beliefs. You already know how to get connected to your intuition, just too often by distraction and constant intellectualisation we miss what intuition is telling us.

The practising of beliefs is for everyone that has the tool of using the mind the opportunity to choose freedom. It's entirely about the one that's practising. It's never about the practice of the other. You're not practising the practice of belief, it is your opportunity to choose. If you choose to live in peace or not depends on you. There is no path that takes away peace when we live intuitively. There will be no way to project to the other and not see it as a mirror. There won't be any moment left where it wasn't you who is the one responsible for the reaction. There won't be any excuses left and no more blaming others. Intuition will tell you exactly what must be done. The one that covers the sound of intuition is the constant speaking mind. The invitation of yourself into yourself is required. It is required stillness.

Living intuitively is an exercise in presence. You know there can be always times where being here as a human can challenge us. The cause is the mind taking us on a journey far away from ourselves. If not at home, not within me, there is space for everything else. When I'm not inside myself, who is it that is inside me? Whoever I invite into myself. Every thought, imagination and envisioning is the opportunity to be a creator or destructor of my inner and outer world. To be the one the deeper dimension of intention expresses, not only in the movement of creation and destruction, I must live from my intuition. Thus if I live from it I integrate it all into myself. I take home what I have excluded from within me. So this is my constant invitation to you to invite yourself into yourself. It is an invitation to me to invite myself into myself. I can invite others into their selves but the only one that I can really invite is myself.

So how does that look in daily life? The depth of wisdom that comes with intuition will show itself behind mirrors of unacceptance. What is a mirror of unacceptance? It is the program that our mind uses as soon as he criticises or judges the moment, any situation from the past or even the future, any person or experience. So here comes the question. But isn't it normal to judge? Don't we need that to survive? Intuition itself already has the greatest relationship with survival instinct. So the judgement itself on just an intellectual level can be a great tool to apply in pragmatic approaches. Not only in survival but to be lead to have a joyful life. The mirror of unacceptance creates segregation of soul and body. 'Living unholistically.' It is me projecting myself into the life of the other, making space within myself, inviting the other into me, instead of inviting myself to me. It's when I don't feel seen, when I don't feel included, when I don't feel respected and cared for. To distinguish between what is threatening really one or another's holistic life and when it is that I have the freedom to choose intuitively what's good for my cells is one of the aims that I'm including what I learned intellectually.

The mirror of unacceptance is when I don't feel loved in any occasion. Take this as a moment to reflect on a situation that you thought wasn't right, should have been different, where you have been treated badly or just didn't enjoy the moment. This is an exercise. An exercise to reflect on any mirror of unacceptance that arises, may it be from the past or the future or even reading this. Invite yourself, be still, be the mirror to yourself, the situation, the person and the experience. So doesn't the other party need to learn as well about the situation and learn that he is also a part of the story? Yes, that will occur naturally. As soon as I open myself up to be, live and act out of my essence and not out of my beliefs, any creature will recognise the presence of soul within your eyes. Even objects that may not seem alive will look back at you. Everything that exists has its own expression of aliveness and soul.

Mirrors of unacceptance are not about changing your opinion and giving the identity another opportunity to be righteous on any subject, it is about opening a space for a deeper dimension to expand experientially beyond intellect.

Maybe the journey isn't so much about becoming anything, maybe it's about unbecoming everything that isn't really you so you can be who you were really meant to be in the first place

—Paolo Coelho

This is an invitation to let your intuition be sensed, heartfelt and expressed free from filters. It is about what it is like to be.

It is about presence.

It is an intellectual and silent practice.

It is about inviting yourself to yourself. Not about inviting the stories that you have about yourself. It is a practice to unpractise all the stories. It is a practice to be still. It is a silent experience.


Is it really that important to live intuitively?

Do I have to be always kind and be aware that everything has a soul?


There are no rules; what I sense is when it comes to believing how things have to be, I lose my life in convictions and stories. I become small-hearted, I become a person that probably doesn't accept others, I become upset if others don't act like I want them to. I lose reality. So my choice is to look at my convictions and see if they give me freedom and peace. If the intention of an interaction or conversation isn't peace I will always lose and hurt myself and then judge others, that they are the reason I'm hurt. That's exhausting for me. So because of that, I live from my intuition. Life happens when I live from the essence of myself. Life shows me what is happening while I am believing convictions and stories and what is happening behind all of those filters and I learn how to play with them rather than be played.

My granny always repeated to me, 'Patrick, a constant dripping wears away the stone' which is a wisdom that I started to understand once I was within me creating and learning how to rewire my cellular connection. Persistence accomplishes things and this in an effortless, joyful state which is accepting and learning to flow with the given.

As soon as I follow the opinions of my inner unacceptance, my heart closes, my chest feels tight, I feel 'mycellf' closing, I want to be righteous. If I open up to the wisdom intuition has to offer and integrate all that the mirrors of unacceptance gift me with, then yes, my heart opens, my chest opens and I have open arms for life. The 10 Point Intuition Cell-Awareness Method on how to live intuitively is the greatest gift I received to unpractise my personal and righteousness beliefs. How else to recognise the mirrors of unacceptance? As soon as something hurts my beliefs, makes me want to convince the other that the opinion is wrong or makes myself as the one who shows the other what cannot be accepted. It's easy to recognise. This mirror itself is very fragile as soon as there is something I'm only projecting and not integrating and it might just be the smallest thing, like a hammer on a mirror. If I hold on to my mirror and fix it with a tape I might not see what an unfiltered, beautiful reality is in the back of it.

The bigger mission and the only way we can create a state of peace within us, outside of us here at this planet and everywhere else is to practise the non-practicing of beliefs that disturb the natural state of joy. When I wasn't able to listen to my inner voice it was like I couldn't reveal myself, neither to me nor to others. I thought I was revealing me but what I was revealing was my story and who I thought I was. This period is my book of wisdom.

From my past selves' perspectives I suffered, I couldn't imagine peace ever in this world. Now my experiences are the greatest source of remembering that it was never the way I thought it was. Seeing reality is what happens if we listen to the sound of intuition. From this deeper dimension, we get the chance to evolve in joy. We will enter in dimensions, which the intellectual mind cannot grasp but where the intellectual mind is the portal to get into it. If I become still and stop, then I find, see and sense what my essence is. I start to reveal myself for myself and for life itself. So often we are scared about the so called dark parts within us but here i need to recognise. I cannot not leave a shadow but I can integrate it the same way I thrive for light. Only when this is the effortless aim is peace realised.

It was needed to evolve and get the update of conscious and intuitive living for something greater which has no words to be described.

The universe is in love with the earth and we are all here in the same boat and can inspire each other to live and experience this deeper dimension. I can use the intellectual mind as a great creator of new concepts and may not find, see or sense what my mission is.

The past is my teacher. My teacher to always remind me that any period that I have lived and I remember is my conviction on how it was and I will never be able to know exactly how it was. Yes, I imagine it and intellectualise it for whatever creation and inspiration and it is still my conviction to remember how it was. The reality I can only experience with my two eyes. That is what I was gifted with. The gift of trusting the truth of intuition. Trusting what intuition shows me. Intuition shows me reality.

Right before I received the opportunity to have a new life I experienced strong changes within my beliefs and my world all around me. It was like all was leaving me. I was leaving me. It was like my world was breaking apart. I couldn't imagine that all the suffering I was going through would lead me to this treasure. What I have received is the greatest gift. I got the chance to see something I only knew from conceptual stories. I got the chance to see the wisdom of a life in peace. The wisdom to know what is not told. The wisdom to invite me to myself and experience what intuition is. I received the call. The call to connect my self to myself, to connect my self to others, to connect others to themselves and connect the self of others to the self of others. It is the call of Intuition. I know that this should be available for everyone.

Because if we all live from our intuition we create a world that evolves in joy. Here the concept of oneness comes close to an intellectual expression. Integrating all that is and seeing whatever comes as a teacher. Does that mean living intuitively is losing individuality and personal choice on when I should be or I should not say what I like and dislike or I should like to be dramatic? So here it's important to recognise intuition as a natural instinct that can always choose the path of peace, freedom and health if it is in fights, a survival situation or any intellectual interaction. For me, it is about doing it from my intuition, doing it from my essence, doing it my way and doing it from all of my heart, and practising to unpractise my mind's beliefs, because only then can I practise the intention of peace.

So what does the mirror of unacceptance do with our physical body? In general, a negative and stressed mind has less beneficial immune responses than a happy mind. What I want to suggest here is to have a look and reflect if rather you choose to believe the angel or devil on your shoulder. The third and deeper option is to live from the core of joy which as you probably already know now is what I sense as intuition. People who generally are happier and satisfied lose themselves less in addictions such as drinking, co-dependency, depression, overeating or smoking and drugs. Trusting the intuition or preferably listening to the positive conceptual thoughts will increase general health and benefit body, mind and soul. It is not to unlisten when we don't feel well or have negative thoughts but the recognition of them and integration.

The emotional and mental state does affect the physical health, therefore it can be beneficial to choose what you ingest to digest. I choose to listen to my intuition. I choose to ingest food that gives me life and is chosen intuitively, I choose to recognise compulsion and turn it into an intuitive way of deciding. I see how intensely an intuitive way of ingesting and consuming alters the state of comfort. I don't only experience it for myself but learn from practitioners that it enhances wellbeing, supports immune responses, helps the body to cope with inflammation eases depression, anxiety and panic attacks. Remember why science is important in my life? Always when I'm not within myself and I feel like I can't choose intuitively, I utilise the wisdom of science and biomedical studies and from there on start to choose. What would that look like? If I am in the supermarket and have the intense need to eat a donut and believe it is my intuition but my physiological psychological state would not benefit from it I could question my beliefs on it. Look at what science is telling me about healthy nutrition and apply it. I would look at food sources that are considered healthy and take three of them and then choose intuitively to what I feel more drawn to.

A thought is harmless unless we
believe it. It's not our thoughts, but
our attachment to our thoughts
that causes suffering. Attaching to a
thought means believing that it's
true, without inquiring. A belief is a
thought that we've been attaching
to, often for years

— Byron Katie

Loving What Is:
Four Questions That Can Change Your Life

All that enters our body may impact the wonderful vehicle we live in. From here on I would love to invite you to have a view on the perspective science gives us. Living intuitively for me is the recognition of individuality and science-given wisdoms to support the body to evolve. The mind mirrors the body very often. For me it is a healthy body that can promote a healthy brain. Body and mind aligned are the gateway to live from the soul. So all that we feel our body with can have an impact on how we experience life. Water, food and cosmetics that we use to nourish the body interact with the natural state or help to regenerate or degenerate. Negative thoughts and beliefs besides food are a cause of depression and a source of where suffering starts from. Having a neutral or positive view on reality eases those conditions. As well stress or anxiety works hand in hand with negative thoughts. If we look at judgement-free acceptance of self there actually are less negative thoughts and less of other negative overwhelming somatic or psychological anxiety experiences. If I become aware where it is that I have not seen myself as a mirror to my actions I create freedom of recognition. What I don't know I cannot integrate thus if I follow my intuition I stop knowing how to practise and learn how to practise the unknown.

Something interesting that I noticed during the last years is that physiological intensification of healing is induced when we look at ourselves and at the other as the person that is standing in front of us. In my research to amplify this book I found this beautiful example of when we are not aware of the psychological stress levels they can decrease the quality of life. This in a range from a normal calm breakfast in a healthy body to a dinner within a body with, for example, rheumatoid arthritis. What I found is that in rheumatoid arthritis negative thought patterns which are mostly correlated to negative or stressful moments or anxiety are an indicator that the physiological degeneration is increasing. When I listen rather to the program of my mind than the individual intuitive wisdom I close the receptivity of tissues and cells within my body. To mirror myself and mirror others' behaviour in me allows me to see where it is that I intensify my suffering. This helps us understand why counselling itself works in reducing anxiety and depression. Can you recall in depression the pull down and its with it coming inflammation? What this wisdom supports for me is that in any condition inspiring the patient to live more intuitively will improve the quality of life. I included this part especially because there is no person I met that with the wisdom of intuition couldn't be supported. One day I was invited to a lady in the western woods of Bavaria; she was in huge pain and couldn't move her joints anymore. I was sitting down with her, and she told me how her life went to hell since she got the diagnosis. She told me, 'Since I know I have that disease my life just isn't valuable anymore.' Can you sense the wisdom behind that? That sentence already blew my mind; we started with this belief that was stuck within her cells and did the 10 together. What came out of it was that when she finished going through the 10 Point Intuition Cell-Awareness Method—actually at that time it was probably more than 10, I didn't yet develop the method so it was more like a back-and-forth feeling and looking into the words that were expressed. So at the end she was laughing. After some days I received a letter where she wrote: 'Patrick, I own now the wisdom to know that I have the disease and know that I don't have it.' Intuition always leads to life lived in more freedom, deep wisdom, greater health and peace itself. My intention while telling you about this story is to inspire you to listen deeper. This will always work if it is not a task. Sometimes I say what intuition is and what it does. But here right now I want to as well tell you with all of my heart that those words that I use I only can describe what it is like. There is no word that I found yet to express the totality of it. What I know for sure is that it makes me be. It gives me presence. It makes me free and gives me peace. There are many practices in this book. Frankly, I want to tell you that they will not work if you need them to work. But they will when you have an open heart to whatever suffering or whatever happiness may arise out of it, because those are the two dualities that wake us up.

Food impacts the way we feel, think and behave in several ways. Looking at traumata, stressful thoughts and obsessive negative thinking it is for me important to mention if we are not aware that individually we have a great power to create images in our mind which can in not even a second change our emotional state. Did you ever see that image of at one side an angel on the shoulder and the other side the devil? For me this is a perfect picture. I decide to which articulation I give

101

weight and living intuitively for me means integrating both and not being identified through them.

You know, so often depression, stress and negative thinking are described as 'just psychological'. So could it be that the consumption of negative news, our own negative thoughts, negative perspectives of others and foods that are extremely pro-inflammatory are a cause of it? Yes, indeed! Inflammation may make us fall quicker into reactive patterns. Having in mind that depression is always accompanied with an inflammatory reaction what would be indicated through an increased production of pro-inflammatory cytokines makes me even more understand why in moments that thoughts would try to inflame me and others lead me at the end of the day to a sadness in every cell all over my body.

To investigate the relationship between processed food consumption and mental health, here explicitly anxiety, I found that there is a significant relationship when we increase the consumption of biophoton-low and processed foods with anxiety. It is important to recognise how food and thoughts impact depression, negative thinking and suffering which are the causes of a stressful, non-empathic behaviour, or a life in empathic distress, which one could say isn't the ground base for a mind at ease. Thus looking beyond the conviction and belief that the external world is

the creator of it may open a door to a freedom that is vaster than imaginable.

How does that help me on my learnings to master intuition? Knowing that all we consume is a factor of how our bodies, brains and feelings are wired we can use one of the oldest wisdoms to clear all that fog of feelings through not consuming. Every cell in our body stores what we experience. If we keep feeding it with loads of information, physical or emotional, there is no time to metabolise all that we experience. So by lowering obsessive consumption of all kinds can be a great start to reset intuition.

God grant me the serenity
to accept the things I cannot change;
courage to change the things I can;
and wisdom to know the difference

—Reinhold Niebuhr Serenity Prayer

# 12. Condition to Create Peace

Why do we all need to look for peace all the time? Why can't we just live without worrying all the time about the whole planet? Yes, you already know it. Because inside hidden it's delicious for the mind to live a little drama. Even the whole body can create an immense sense of self out of those little or big romantic dramas that we invite into our life. I want to elaborate on peace and the condition to create peace. As soon as we are born we gain the opportunity to express ourselves individually with our birth-given identity. Social and ethical values cage our experience of being human and filter it through beliefs. Those beliefs cover the naturally given intuitive wisdom and bring us away from the state of being individual and turn us into idealistic statues that can't move out of the imagined world. This creates a fragmented self-image by only inviting beliefs which evaluate what is peace and what isn't. What peace looks like and how it doesn't look. It creates such a fragmentation that it causes the condition for peace which shows a never-ending downwards spiral where peace is never achievable because there is always an effort to find new opportunities to be taken to make things better than they are.

It is an illusion that peace comes from convincing someone that by adopting other beliefs peace can be created through a conceptual way of behaviour which identifies with your personal self-image or everything that comes with your name. Illusion in its roots has the meaning of 'to play, mock, trick' which I find beautifully accurate. As an Illusion doesn't need to be unenjoyable only but yes it can bring any enjoyable feelings with it. I feel that an intuitive approach is the one that flows with inspiration and curiosity rather than an effort of needing to correct. The energy that I receive from intuition is so crystalline that it opens a space where peace is created as soon as I allow myself to integrate the parts that I don't consider peaceful. If I push away what doesn't feel peaceful for me and separate it as a misidentification which has the same frequency but just mirrored downwards than identification I'm trapped in the belief of peacism, if that word even exists. I don't want to convince you how peace should look. I would love to invite you here to experience it in your personal and individual way what peace is for you. How peace looks for you.

At this very moment humans are evolving from the condition to create peace to a state of peace. Why this need to create peace? In childhood we are often caged to act in the way that social and ethical values demand. Which may lead into a need of self-evaluation. The self-evaluation here can be taken in later age through identification of a socially well-seen honourable behaviour and turns the attitude into a exhausting self-identification. The exhausting self-identification is a mechanism that puts oneself and others in a constant valuation of victimhood which creates the need to evolve to peace and push away or argue against everything that doesn't create peace. Or making oneself as honourable to show how bad others are and then turning into the trap of showing how unpeaceful others are which is already an identification of the opposite of peace.

Everything that I push away from myself and don't integrate like it would be my best friend I split it apart, I deny it and I devalue it and then it becomes a Trojan horse identity pattern. Where I give my attention is where energy flows. I invite you here to invite yourself and then naturally effortless be intuitively. Like the sun and the moon which both are guides and reflect light to the earth and give space to the night as well. From a deeper perspective there is nothing that doesn't shine the light of consciousness, might it be day or night. Meeting humans with an open heart and a life lived from intuition and what's beyond intuition seems even to shine through the physiological body. This what you sense, feel and see is the wave of consciousness expanding and being beyond identification and beyond misidentification.

Peace is subjective and objective as long as I try to understand, force or create it. But if I just follow the flow of my intuition it will just be effortless. It will just happen.

It's my invitation to you to consider peace as a experience lived when all parts are integrated that like and dislike in the attitude of others. Wholeness is only reality when I see reality through not only my inner eye but with the two eyes that have been given to me. When I'm aware of what happens within me and see the parts that I split apart, see when it is that I am not creating peace, I can use this awareness to get clarity and call back home what I have pushed away. it is the invitation of me into myself. That is intuition.

Most of you reading this are already on the so-called path of peace and understand that peace can be created, yes, but consider only through an intuitive, holistic, empathic approach towards oneself and others. Not by segregation. Living intuitively is the integration of everything that appears to be dark or appears to be light and see what's beyond those concepts.

The urge to change the world and just believing convictions of how the habitants of this planet are and how they now should be or in which state the planet is and how it should or shouldn't be cages not only myself into a world that can't evolve because I constantly cast a spell repeating this cage, but it cages the others as well; the mind doesn't give them freedom in the imagination.

They are labelled the ones that are not creating peace ... you know, the universe always delivers what we are convinced of. If I invite myself to myself then it is that I see reality as it is. Then I see me as the one who inhabits the power of creating peace within me.

Okay, something for daily life. Imagine some children playing with toys in a room and they are just making a mess and leaving it without organising it again. Let's say a parent would just keep repeating, 'You are making a mess, you are not caring about your toys, you are having no responsibility, this all is a chaos, clean this mess now.' That's as one example the way education is unconsciously taught in TV shows. You think this way the children will learn how to organise? You are right, of course not ... How would it look if you would invite the children after they played into the room again and talked to them, from the heart, explaining? And having a conversation telling why being more careful, more quiet or having empathy is important for general good living together and then call them to action?

All is a mirror and if I'm not reacting out of my heart, being loving and caring in the way that I act, then once I want them to respect my realm they can't because I'm projecting it.

Only by being connected to my inner wisdom and the source of consciousness do I free the world from being the way I cast it to be. Consciousness will always give you a glimpse of when it is that you are not following your intuition. It will hurt you, it will make you want to be righteous, it will make you want to change the other, it will make you leave yourself and inflame yourself or others. This is a call from your consciousness to realise this isn't peace you were striving for, this was a belief you were enslaving someone else and yourself with.

Here is a practice. The next time you come into a situation where you feel the urge of creating peace, connect to yourself. Invite yourself into your body. Feel all your cells from head to toe. Then with this energy you will open unfiltered reality and act out of your intuition. Your intuition always wants you to be whole, be in peace and be free.

Intuition and reality are the same for me. It is to see what is real and what is filtered through beliefs. If I connect to my inner guidance, the sound of intuition, I will be already enough to inspire others to be the inspiration for others for following the route that's beyond peace and war. Only if I integrate all and see life as a mirror to myself. See where it is that if I believe in a world full of war where do I have the same war within me, with others, where is it that I'm fighting with the external world the same way I'm fighting with my struggles. If I allow myself to be radical, honest, here I shine consciousness into me and into the outer world. I use the

10 Point Intuition Cell-Awareness Method to lift my
filtered reality.


Recalling the topic of depression which is for me always
when I press myself or others down. A funny thing is
that almost all antidepressants have special anti-
inflammatory effects. It seems that these anti-
inflammatory compounds could augment the efficacy of
antidepressants. I sensed within me that the same occurs
whenever I fast, there is less fire within me. The body
gets even colder, as funny as it sounds. In my
perspective, in moments where my body has to deal with
lots of inflammation I can take a couple of days and
switch into less consumption of my thoughts, foods and
other things that I feel are inflaming me. Clear body,
clear mind.


I want you to imagine how a cell looks like for you. As
the cell is the basis of an living organism. They are very
flexible in their shape, their inner organisation they
know when and how to be responsive in their
environment, they have this wisdom to fully sustain all
life on this planet.


That's a wisdom that's older than 2000 years. The
ancient Chinese yin and yang concept is a simple
teaching to explain the principle of how life works. The
yin and yang concept refers to two opposite forces which
are mutually dependent on each other. They live

intertransformably. Beautiful to see in the Taiji Diagram. Their playful interconnection is therefore seen as the maintenance of the dynamic balance in life.

Knowing that we can access as well external wisdom to amplify it with our experiences, I would love to emphasise how inflammation, considering inflammation as not only a cause of mental instability but physical instability, is when life is not integrated with both mutual forces as the yin and yang concept would explain it. There is even the yin and yang of inflammation. I often speak about inflammation as something to inflame our minds but it actually is a very important process within our body. Even more important in moments where the physiology is threatened. Inflammation itself is an extremely protective response to infection within the body. Know that many conditions are the product of an inflammation. To explain that, inflammation can lead to an autoimmune condition such as we had above— rheumatoid arthritis. Those include as well tissue damage, which is a key element in almost every chronic health condition. Those conditions can go from heart conditions to diabetes, and furthermore, dysregulation in the normal process of ageing. Fascinating, isn't it?

So seeing yin and yang as a concept within the human body, traditional Chinese medicine promotes that good health is directly connected to the harmony between both those yin and yang qualities. One is the physiological body and the psychological mind. If body and mind get into disharmony, then it is when one of those two qualities is considered to be deficient in something or has within it what would be called emptiness. That's what I correlate to intuition. When I don't invite myself into myself, that's when I feel disconnected to myself, that's when I feel empty. Emptiness, looking at it like a human condition, can be in a way sensed as boredom, disconnection, no social interactions that are filling me with joy and filling the other, and even apathy. Emptiness often comes with a lot of friends. Depression, feeling loneliness, inability to feel pleasure in normally pleasurable activities, despair which is the absence of hope. Some other friends that come with emptiness are very often mental disorders which include schizoid personality disorder and attention deficit hyperactivity disorder. The list is even longer: post-trauma, attention deficit hyperactivity disorder, borderline personality disorder and schizotypal personality disorder are all known to be linked to inflammation.

Consider that intuition is the opportunity to be guided to a harmonious life. With the information in this book you can find your own truth and inner wisdom of what health means to you. Conditions seen as problems may take away the power it beholds to teach. Every problem needs energy so that it can exist. So allow yourself to change from that perspective to a solution.

# 13.  The Arguing Trap

Do you feel the hesitation of arguing or even a need to argue about everything? General social values feed the fear of arguing or the fear of not having argued. What I mean with this is the creation of unhealthy hierarchic which leads to alienation of self. As soon as we identify with the fear of expressing what we feel or the urge to argue about a situation we thought the opposite side should have been acting differently about, we create a gap of connectedness. This universe is an interacting, living organism where no other thing than oneness exists. Separation exists only in the identifying mind which constantly traps itself with Trojan horses.

Why is it that we constantly have the urge to please or displease someone instead of living intuitively which is the only way to live a life in peace?

It is the concept of being disconnected rather than realising that in this universe there is no such thing as connection or disconnection as it is all beyond those concepts.

It's not only the feeling of a gap of connection with others that leads us to please others. As soon as we decide rather to evaluate and act out of the social ethical behaviour and egoic self-identification of belief we cut apart what our inner guide is telling us. But isn't arguing bad? If I connect to my inner guide I will be able to communicate my soul's wishes without the need to argue with myself or with others. Any arguments inherit a shaming mechanism to oneself or others.

How to communicate my soul's calls?

Take a pen and write down what it is that the other person wants from you.

For example:

*My partner wants me to work more and bring more attention to things that I do.*

Now please write down what it is that you want from your partner. For example:

*I want my partner to care about himself and not be so needy.*

Now please find the mirror of when it is that your partner wants what you want and when it is that you want what your partner wants.

Now take your wants and turn it to the opposite. For example:

*I don't want my partner to care about himself and I want him to be needy.*

Now find a moment where this applies.

Now do the same from what your partner wants. For example:

*My partner doesn't want me to work more and doesn't want me to give more attention to things that I do.*

Now reflect and find a moment where this applies in the relationship between you.

The last step will be to do this with the same quality of attention and presence before or while in a conversation. See it as an exercise to unpractise what you believe about your partner. Utilise your eyes to recognise soul in your partner. Use your eyes to unpractise your beliefs and you will give any relationship the space to be new whenever you meet.

# 14. In the Beginning Was The Word

The word as itself is used on this beautiful planet to exchange information and transmit whatever moves us. Every word creates a symphonic vibration which inherit values and intentions which than may be received from others. Those vibrations, those words carry with them a unique quality and value for the receiver and for the expresser. If we have the opportunity to use this ability of transmitting thoughts into words and then again words into thought we get the wonderful orchestra of exchange. Words and sound are vibrations that carry in their frequencies' knowledge that the other and oneself's mind can then interpret. If I tell you that there is an angel behind you hugging you and caring about you, you see that in your imagination, if I tell you that in your living room is a flying unicorn with purple wings and rainbow teeth eating a strawberry shortcake with a wooden spoon, you can see that in your imagination. You don't only see it but you can sense and feel as well from all that the imagination creates.

How easy it was, you just made yourself feel it, think about it and see it by using words. Those are examples that probably won't make you feel uncomfortable or stressed out. But most of the time if the mind is not in tune with intuition it starts to constantly label and think how things should and how things shouldn't be. The mind even argues and fights with what happened in the past, to make sure there is even a chance where the righteousness can be felt even more intensely. So what does that have to do with the word? It is my thought and belief about the word that I or the other speak that shapes my world. There are many languages on this planet and yes, you probably have guessed it, every language has its own quality of vibration. Every person who speaks at least a second language may have experienced that words and expressions speaking another language make you feel, sense and see things differently. It might even change the attitude and behaviour. Words that are spoken create what we think reality is. Words that are spoken can show us reality as it is. Words that are spoken speak for themselves. It's each one's interpretation that creates the quality of the experience. Each language has its individual social and ethical values which shape our beliefs. But let me tell you, there is a space between words, between beliefs, between cultures and between individual reality. That's the space where the word of peace happens.

Love is freedom. How to have commitment and have freedom?

Love for me is the covered word for freedom. The opposite of love is fear for me. All that isn't freedom and consists of fear I can question for myself and look beyond what I think love is and gives me. Fear of losing a loved one, fear of being betrayed, fear of losing an created identity, fear of losing consciousness, fear of losing material things, fear of being shamed, fear of terrorism, fear of not being loved. It is the identity that fights with freedom. Any relationship is ultimate love, we can choose if the experience is in a joyful or suffering way. Allow yourself in any relationship to invite yourself instead of the beliefs of how the opposite or you should be. To love is to be in freedom and allow others to be free. To compromise can be the romanticism that gives life a little fire which we all love from time to time.

Here is a little practice. If there should be a relationship with your partner, family member, friend or work colleague that is drawing your energy away use it as a portal to understand your soul's plan. It is important here to reflect not to project!

Find a person or moment that is drawing your energy away. Reflect, be as real to yourself as you can be and look where it is that you aren't feeling freedom towards the moment or the other.

Take notes and write them down...

Now look at your notes. Read them. Please find an example where the exact same applies to the counterpart and write it down.

Listen to your heart; it is the only path to see reality, it is living intuitively.

So here is an essential question. Will this be the cure for every relationship? What I can tell you is that it's not to decide. It's for the one who thinks what and who am I to decide if I believe the thought or if I look at reality? It can't be my decision to cure a relationship. So the question is, if I give total freedom do I still compromise? The thing that I compromise is to live from my inner wisdom that gives me freedom, health and peace. All those three beautiful virtues are expressed in every person individually. So how could I compromise to the idea of freedom if freedom is different for everyone? Just to compromise, to have rules, social and ethical values? If love is coming into your experience isn't it important to compromise to someone's love?

Does that give you freedom to compromise to someone's love? If love comes into my life and I have to compromise I ask myself where is it that love is. The stillness behind this question makes intuition take over. It makes love take over. When I allow my intuition to raise I'm possessed by love.

Of soul you shall never find boundaries,
not if you track it on every path; so
deep is it's cause


—Heraclitus

# 15. Connection

How do I perceive connection? Connection is the permanent state of just being. Being connected to all that is manifested, to all that I manifested. Real connection is nothingness and everything. What is the temple of god? It is the body as well, yes. Who resides within the body? Yes, it is me. Who am I connected to then? Yes, to god, as god created humans in his image. Being the temple of god, being the space in the temple, being one who lives in the temple, being the space that the temples lives in. Being the space where all comes from and the space where nothing has its home. Being all, being infinite, being all that's before and beyond infinity. The word god has different literal meanings. Two that stand out for me are:

'that which is invoked' or 'to call'

'libation' or 'that which is libated upon'

The first one refers to me as the opportunity to invite myself into my cells. I call myself back from all places.

From my thought about work, family, house, car, problems, moments in future and past. I invoke myself into me to then be able to express the inner wisdom the my source of being has to offer.

The second one the liberation is for me a perfect example on what intuition does what god is, what I do when I follow my inner guide. It is to 'pour as an offering'. I pour myself as an offering. To be myself I need to invite me and invoke me into myself that from there on I'm the effortless offering towards others.

As my dear friend Thomas Singer told me, intuition is to think with God's mind. Besides sensing what he expressed this may be a beautiful intellectual understanding to make it a little more romantic and as well understandable in the context of the book.

Intuition serves as a gentle, freeing and deep personal opinion to connect to what your soul is asking for, especially on what benefits the general well-being. Intuition is derived as well from cellular experience that's not only individual and cultural but goes beyond this individual physical incarnation. It is like a deep-rooted wisdom, which forms the basis of individual intuition. It can be seen as well as the individual guide for optimal evolution. This intuitive wisdom contributes to the beneficial evolution that intuition initiates. It is constantly flowing and changing. New conceptual understandings are embodied and suggested by intuition. Intuition provides us with a non-intellectual knowledge that leads the direction for a peaceful, free and healthy environment. All concepts of interaction that come from intuition are influenced for an outcome that is always good. This includes conceptual choices of food, drinks, directions and decisions in general. You could look at it like a freely accessible library that doesn't need to be directly accessed with the intellect. It just flows through everyone and everything.

Our body and all cells are always interested in progress. So if we listen to the intuition we will support this progress; even a false guess that comes from only the conceptual mind may lead to progress. Intuition also plays a major role in the evolution of future predicting.

The stillness that allows intuition to speak with us is often not only covered by the judgements and assumptions that we have, it actually gets overheard by all the information that we consume during the day. It is from nutritional science, health advocates, movies, Netflix, spiritual wisdoms, pragmatic approaches or guidelines on how to live. All these guides are wonderful and amazing tools that can help us approach a whole life, but what we often miss by following guidelines is listening to our individual intuition that always wants us to be healthy, joyful and in peace. The gateway to access the intuition is not found by focusing on the external world that much, but being aware on what is through being present in the body. Health for me does not depend on a physiological label or state.

Let me give you an example on how to elaborate with consumption. Not only does all that we eat define our health but all that we read, hear, think and talk about impacts our general health, at least till we are aware of it. After my experience in Mallorca I started to notice how thoughts and intentions in my past were just to make it right for someone else or me. In the beginning was the word and it is powerful. Every word has an intention. What is the power of intention? The meaning that I found in this word is stretching one's own and others' purpose to see what purpose will come out and with what it started when I began to stretch. What I found was that intention seems to be similar to a thought which then called one to go into action. The thoughts which are targeted to an end can therefore affect not only human beings, animals and plants but all living things, from a big elephant to an unicellular organism.

There is an emission of light particles which seems to be one of the mechanisms that the intention produces as its outcome, called as well biophotons. That is what I see as the light of life that every organism emits. Did you know that every organism emits a never-ending and constant current of photons as a means to give direct, instantaneous and nonlocal emission of signals from one part of the body to another and to the external world? I started to research more about this topic as for me objects get aliveness when intention or attention is guided to it. So biophotons have their home in the intracellular DNA structure. Every organism in this third reality has an intention. This intention manifests itself as magnetic energy or as an electric energy producing an ordered process of flowing of photons. Every intention operates as a highly consistent frequency which has the capacity to alter the molecular structure of matter.

Did you ever have an intention where you felt you wanted to do something and then didn't listen to what your intuition told you? So in this world there is no such thing as second chance, but other chance. That the intention of an action can be effectively manifested it is necessary to sense and know when it is the right time to do so. The intuitive timeline radar is my inner guide for that. As well as this energy coherently flowing through us, it flows through others. All living beings are mutually synchronised to this planet whether aware of it or not. We are in symbiosis with this planet and even with every magnetic energy. Energy of intention or the power of the word and the thought behind it alters the environment we live in. In the beginning was the word and it is powerful. If I become aware and honour my beliefs by integrating them then my state of consciousness can induce spontaneous cures or even interact when I send a prayer to a loved one, which works like remote healing. Every intention to heal or the conviction of sickness and other conditions is crucial in the efficacy of healing. I have seen so often that thoughts, convictions and beliefs change our inner biology and receptivity for intuitive medicine. Know that there is a space between intention of healing or having a condition. This space is the ultimate source of wisdom for being whole beyond concepts.

What we occupy our minds with will be like a main mantra. If this mantra is just a copy of a guideline from someone else or their beliefs, we will be led by the intellectual and always judging mind. When I speak about judging mostly I mean the judgement that creates social disconnection. But if we clear all those beliefs and go back to the core of intuition the mantra will arise naturally and full of grace. Each body has an individual sound and an individual language. The only one who can know what is best for you is you, living intuitively. What if I think I'm living from my intuition and I'm still not healthy, free and in peace? Is my intuition not working correctly? Intuition never fails, but the egoic identity always loves to fight with what really is. It wants always a new and more complicated way to keep the mind busy. When we are in that spiral of only intellect we all love a drama and a little complication. So here again my concept of intuition. It nourishes, loves and brings to peace all that exists.

What would be a good example on how to distinguish intuition from beliefs when it comes to consumption? Let's say you're just getting home from work, had a successful day and planned a couple of days ago to have a healthy dinner with friends. But suddenly when you arrive home, you feel just wonderfully comfortable, but you also would enjoy the evening with your friends. How to choose? What would your intuition like to show you? I want you to imagine the two options: staying at home or going out with friends having a healthy dinner. Okay then, maybe a thought comes: *Okay, cool, so I'm going to get up, dress, meet my friends, because we already planned it, and I will also hear all the news about what happened during the last week.*

But then you hear your inner call just asking for stillness; maybe you are not even hungry but decide to join your friends because you're going to have a healthy vegan dinner. So here it would be a belief that meeting friends would have a higher value for you on a level of intellectual and physical consumption. This can also be a turnaround that your intuition is telling you. Go and experience life outside, but then you don't go because of beliefs of what would and could happen. Intuition if we look closer here is not intellectual. It will indeed lead you to a greater outcome, with greater I mean effortless, but not by the use of the intellectual mind.

So with the easy practice of arriving in the body, getting aware of what is really happening in front of our two eyes and listening to the non-judgemental inner world, we use intuition as a guide for a life in peace, health and freedom. Intuition can judge to guide you in what is giving you freedom but it will judge without making you judge. This is actually not only for you. If you experience your intuition and live from the source of your inner wisdom you can access external wisdom as well. It will get into symbiosis with the core of the inner views with ease and through that it can bring joy to all beings by living reality in this present moment.

## Isolation, relation and intuition

Often we tend to feel alone, disconnected, not understood because of all the terrifying things that are done to us or to others.

To compromise or to not compromise are the only reasons to feel isolation. To feel disconnected and to not live on a harmonious wave creates segregation.

Fight, aggression, anger, jealousy, fear and crime are rooted in the isolation sphere. You can imagine it like that if a person doesn't intellectually understand another person or doesn't want to accept the self it starts to create a sphere where only the egoic beliefs have the chance to survive. This non-acceptance and not understanding starts to be programmed in childhood trough ethical and social belief systems. The sphere of isolation is so thick that it can be the lightfire for any disharmony in relations and even every crime. There is no crime that is not rooted in the isolation sphere which is ultimate segregation in the individual egoic mind. I can commit only a crime to my commitment, a crime to society or a crime towards myself and others when I can't sense the external or my internal world as a part of me.

Anger itself is blocked energy that is expressed through the intellect because one has not been aware that one isn't the anger but the actor that is expressing anger. By believing the mind that there is such a thing as not being seen, respected, not having enough resources, not having the chance to have a good life, even an advocate for something which the person has done socially or ethically wrong/differently in the past we step into the trap of the isolation sphere. The mind itself creates such a strong imagination on how terrible the external world is that all that's beyond the sphere is very foggy, almost not visible. In this world there are many things that the mind can consider as terrible. But if I trust the negative thinking mind and can't see my connection and how I isolate myself from others and myself that is what creates the inner war. The war that wants to be fought is not to the external world but yes, all that anger is an inner call to destroy the sphere.

Please recognise that anger, which is a crime to oneself and others, is a call of the inner world to tell the person experiencing it to unpractise the beliefs that created the sphere. Even after crimes to oneself and others it is essential to understand that one is never the story of the past and not the imagination of the future. The meaning of crime can be translated into 'wickedness, sin'. If a human decides after a punishment, either from self-punishment, relationships or governmental, that one self is not essential the story of what has been before, that is it when the sphere dissolves. That is the opportunity to experience connection which is the ultimate craving of humanity. That is when every person gets the opportunity to start a new life in any given moment.

No man ever steps in the same river twice, for it's not the same river and not the same man

—Heraclitus

Practise to transform anger, segregation and isolation.

Please travel in time with your mind to a moment where you are or have been angry.

To a moment where you wanted justice to happen.

To a moment where justice needed to take place.

Now at this moment look at how you feel connected to the other person.

Sense how the connection feels. Maybe you feel that you are segregating, that you are hateful, feeling lots of anger, maybe you are upset, you feel that you are unkind or feel that you are aggressive. Take a couple of moments for any answer to arise.

How does that make you feel in your body?

How can this make others feel about them and you?

Now reflect and imagine how you and the other would act in the same moment if there would not have been this specific feeling of segregating, that you are hateful, feeling lots of anger, maybe you are upset, you feel that you are unkind or feel that you are aggressive.

Take a couple of moments for any thought or answer that might arise.

What would you be doing in this moment without the excessive expression of those feelings?

How would you communicate with the counterpart?

Would you even communicate to the counterpart?

How would the quality of your experience change and how would this change your relation toward the other, and towards your current situation in this moment right now?

What would you wish to you? Here you would be speaking to you like you would be in the role of your best friend or maybe a person that cares and loves you. What would be a wish from this person that loves you to you?

I wish you that ...

Now take the same sentence and connect again to the counterpart from the beginning of the exercise and wish them the same from you.

And last but not least, do it for you. Don't forget yourself. Wish it from yourself to yourself.

This is a practice to understand the mind's visions and see how emotions can be understood on a deeper level. It can be my individual choice to live a life in connection but only if I step back from what I have learned from social and ethical values that is rooted in society. I can if I step into myself and not be only what I believe but be something bigger than that. It's the opportunity to be. To create, to inspire and innovate. There is no human on this planet that can't be the greatest teacher when my thoughts are challenged and I'm getting reactive. Only when I know that the cause of it can be the mind can I learn to understand it and listen to the wisdom of intuition which gives me freedom wherever I am.

Knowing and understanding each individual's emotions can make one understand between what the feeling of an emotion is and the difference of self-identification with the belief or conviction that 'I am upset, angry, nervous, stressed' (I am the emotion). It gives freedom and space to unpractise the practice of emotional identification. It makes us understand the difference between the self and the sense of self that one has. This balance is essential for a holistic and therefore healthier life. It gives us the freedom to interact from a space of choice. If it is believed that one is the emotion, 'I am angry', it cages one in a belief that has no space for freedom and peace left. If I open my heart and listen to the wisdom of intuition I can understand my individual physiological experiences and experience them rather than make them who I am. It is a shift from I am angry towards I'm feeling anger and understanding where it comes from. Like my friend OCEAN always mentions: 'Patrick my anger today is in a dramatic mood.' What a wisdom... It's the invitation of the self to understand where it is that I wasn't giving freedom to me and the other as all is a reflection of myself. It helps me therefore to see the feeling of angry as any other physiological experience without feeding the fire but yes, letting it burn, experiencing it and then integrating it to understand if I'm on the path my heart has planned for me.

So often emotions are pushed apart and from all of my heart once again please let yourself experience and understand the wisdom that emotions hold. They contain information that is subconsciously processed and hidden behind the filters that hold back what intuition wants to tell us. Understanding the emotion by having the freedom to react strengthens our intuitive intelligence. It's a clearer experience of reality and does not segregate negative and positive thoughts but integrates both and sees them neutrally as a source of valuable content and information. This information helps me understand my individuality of physiological and emotional reactions.

# 16.  Feeling 'Onecellf' and 'Othercellfs'

Living from intuition will release our natural given empathic gift. Empathy is for me to experience and understand what others are sensing, feeling, being receptive of their perspectives and going through and having the knowledge to distinguish what my feelings are and what comes from the other or what is simply my imagination. Intuition initiates empathy, both to recognise what others are feeling and to be more discerning, which leads to a more peaceful outcome at understanding others. Missing intuition is missing empathy and living a present life. Through intuition we can become more aware of our own emotions which is important to build compassion. With listening to our core we can increase empathy by developing mental habits of distinguishing what is a belief and what is reality and my intuition telling me. It's an invitation to experience the beauty of life, a chance of seeing similarities and offering kindness. Invite your intuition to arise in your mind constantly and it will become a mental habit. What we think, we become, because in the beginning was the word!

Many of our filters keep us away from having the experience and feeling of being connected to ourselves and others. We all know that in stressful moments we often forget that the person right next to us is just a human too. We have an instinctive need to connect even more if we aren't connected to the intuition. Whenever we experience anger, emotional pain, cell-closing judgements and closed-heartedness it can be seen like a wound that wants to be cared for. It can happen when we look for connection through similarities. We naturally all love to connect, as we sense we are interconnected and often the mind hides with romantic and dramatic stories this what is beyond connection and disconnection. it doesn't matter if it's through physical contact or an intellectual context like conversation, arguments, fights or inspirational discussions. Those come all from the drawing force to connect. Living from intuition, we naturally get empathic and connect beyond intellectual and physical occasions.

This interconnectedness is a non-practicing practice therefore if the mind takes over and intuition is filtered it's often misunderstood and misapplied. Whenever there is only good seen or only evil in one entity that is indeed the truth for the one who experiences the believe and it is as well a little part of the truth.

Empathy is not critical pragmatism and explanation why and how we act the way we do, or speculating in therapeutical or psychological terms or on psychological motivations. When we judge or over intellectualize we are actually not interconnected and we create rather disconnection. If we judge in a way that the cells are not opening up we are not understanding it. The same happens with intellectualizing food choices.

Without the belief of what is healthy and what isn't healthy we gain back the freedom of intuitive choice. Like a child that naturally picks from a basket the fruit it feels like eating. There is no intellectualisation of which fruit is higher in sugar, where the most antioxidants are and what protects from ageing. Listening to the intuition will naturally give the best outcome possible for your fabulous, individual body in this incarnation. Concepts are great to create a general pathway on how to live healthy. Out of these concepts to get into the real intuitive choices is freedom. Intuition wants the best for everyone; maybe that is why it is a freeing and peace-bringing experience. It seeks universal harmony and peace. Yes, it does! Trust in your intuition; it is always there for you. Even if you don't listen for a while, it will still be there. Unconditional and non-judgemental. It will show you the light and darkness of essence within everything. It will enlighten your thoughts and beliefs. Intuition will lighten your life. It will release your inner wisdom.

# 17.  Healthism Trap

Exhausted worrying about health,

overthinking which supplements to take,

conceptualise what shall be eaten and considered to be not eaten,

what food has a better frequency and what lowers your energetic field,

getting stressed out how to exercise,

forcing yourself to perform yoga or meditate,

stressed out what others think when you are not on a highly healthy track,

how to look younger and live longer?

That's the healthism trap.


It will be the healthism trap that I will elaborate on and how to get back to the intuitive knowledge about health that our cells carry.

The healthism trap can lead to chronic stress where the individual is only valued through the belief of how health should look. This stress inflames the mood and therefore it as well inflames the physiology. Research demonstrates that inflammation which is induced by stressful thoughts leads the healthy cells to say goodbye. It is this that can lead to chronic conditions from depression to heart conditions to fatigue and arthritis. Notice that inflammation is a contributor to almost every condition in older adulthood. There can be so many moments, experiences and traumas that make us feel small-hearted, and the chest feels tight where we feel contraction within us. These contractions create physiological blockages which can be a big contributor to all kinds of physiological and psychological conditions. All of our emotions here having a deeper focus on stressful ones are involved in biochemical consequences which can determine our health. I invite you here that if there should be a moment where health is that low that it is taking away your opportunity to live a joyful life consider the wisdom that science has to offer.

Let's have a look at what stress and mood have to do with inflammatory condition processes. It's essential to see how our beliefs shape the way our cells interact within the physiology and understand that stress that is not properly metabolised leads to stuck physiological responses that attack the state of homeostasis which is the stable optimal functioning activity equilibrium in physiology.

It's about intuitive individualism recognising not only health self-shaming but the shaming of others.

I want to invite you to reflect on the dilemmas that can arise when we get into the healthism trap where we constantly judge everything to be healthy or unhealthy and worry when not in the role of being healthy.

So what is the healthism trap? It's the constant preoccupation with healing health and health improvement. A never-ending intellectual practice of achievement of well-being. It is a belief system which sees health like something that needs to be achieved constantly with the responsibility of the one that's the achiever on a way of rating the personal practice and call to put health above everything else. It's a practice which through the modification of lifestyle we should get healthier. The healthism trap ignores that health is not only a physical or mental matter, it is a holistic approach to being whole. With a constant self-criticism that nothing is healthy enough. So how does the World Health Organization describe health?

'As a state of complete physical, mental and social well-being.'

In general, it's a good guideline but are we less when we do not have one of these traits? Identification with health can lead to improved health or lead to identification of a health image in one's mind which protects the egoic self-identification. This can lead to self-blaming and as well blaming others for not doing their best on being healthy if we aren't aware of it.

The healthism trap can even cage us to live according to a certain belief system on how we should eat, which mostly is backfired from biomedical research. I want to invite you here please to consider that science is the intellectual development of intuition. Intuition itself has a knowledge that is incompatible when it is about understanding the individuality of each human's physiological constitution. Every human has an individual physiological constitution which cannot be caged into a belief system that comes with a diet guideline when it is regarding health. So question your convictions and beliefs if you are eating plant-based, keto, pescatarian, vegan, vegetarian or any other because of a belief or because you felt intuitively into it.

What else is it that needs to be considered? The stress parameters of the healthism trap which I just elaborated about cause chronic stress and this promotes pathogenesis degeneration rather than salutogenesis healing and regeneration; chronic stress is a biochemical perturbation which not only could promote cancer growth by the direct induction of uncontrolled cell proliferation but as well cause other conditions.

Those biochemical perturbations compromise homeostasis to the degree that even prevents spontaneous recovery. Conditions whose development have been linked to both stress and inflammation include cardiovascular dysfunctions, as well as mentioned cancer, diabetes, autoimmune syndromes, and mental disorder or illness such as depression and anxiety disorders. Stress interacts with the behaviour of cytokines which are regulators of interactions with infection, inflammations, trauma and immune responses.

Some of those so-called cytokines act degenerative and make the condition worse—they are called proinflammatory—whereas some others can support to reduce inflammation and promote self-healing which are anti-inflammatory. The ones called proinflammatory cytokines which are induced as well through stress can be involved in the development of the abovementioned chronic stress and as well depression. Typical symptoms of extreme anxiety, stress and depressive disorders could also be the withdrawal of social interactions, decreased physical activity, mood, and cognitive alterations and fatigue. What we think and believe is what the cells are going to express. The mind and its convictions are participators which act as degenerators or regenerators of the biological life. Those are adaptive responses, and they are all orchestrated by cytokines, and this is important for the physical body as it is meant to divert an individual from ordinary activities to save energy and hold it for recovery.

It's a natural response of the body to keep the frequency low to be able to recover and get into a state of regeneration. Stress itself needs to be experienced and metabolised totally. What does that mean that I start stressing myself out? Let me say it another way: often when we get into stress mode we don't take even a breath to realise where the stress comes from. There can be only one overall reason for a life that's too stressful or even promotes burnout. What is that? Yes, it is a life that is led by convictions and beliefs rather than the wisdom of intuition. Remember, intuition always makes you invite situations to be experiences and this integration is the portal to peace.

So here comes the healthism trap again: an individual, if he is to be considered healthy, should not suffer from any condition. So if I suffer from any condition, I already tell myself I'm not healthy, leading to the self-degenerative nocebo effect instead of the regeneration through belief, also called placebo.

Most of you probably know what placebo is. It is taking a sugar pill instead of the actual medication and the belief in the benefits is the force that actually intensifies the natural self-healing ability. So placebo is the physiological response to the beliefs. The beauty of the word placebo if translated reflects the unconditional, never-ending love to keep going that our body has even in the most degenerative states. Placebo means 'I will please'.

Placebo and nocebo are the creating or destructing power that we all have just by casting one thought. The destructing twin of the placebo is the nocebo.

Never heard of nocebo? Let me explain ... Nocebo is when a person is conditioned to expect a response negatively, and anticipate degenerative effects from acting not according to beliefs or ethical and social values.

The placebo effect or natural self-healing power has been widely researched. Relatively new studies have shown that nocebo can have a stronger effect than placebo. So if I don't believe or understand a concept of health or if I am acting out of the healthism trap, this can cause a downwards spiral frequency where the beliefs and convictions degenerate me. It has strong physiological effects and can reduce health by just believing the imagination that something isn't healthy. I invite you to look at scientific findings somewhat neutral than with emotional response. It is the space between placebo and nocebo that can be the power that is effortless.

There have even been studies where it was demonstrated that patients who are anxious or expect pain during a procedure feel more pain because of this negative expectation. It's crucial to understand that a negative expectation as well reduces focus, disrupts the neural processing of new learnings and filters reality. It takes away individuality and cages in a concept of how to be, as an individual, healthy. Here is the call to live intuitively and if I would be lost in ideas to choose scientific research as a guide to get back to natural health.

Please invite yourself now to see where it is that you are telling others that a specific diet or lifestyle isn't healthy. Everything is a mirror and as long as I show others what is and isn't healthy from an emotional, reactive response I do act out of convictions. When I have a conversation that is inspiring others and inspiring me to show each person where the health in the other is rather than the illness, then I allow myself to heal as well.

Every person that I consider as ill and use them to unconsciously shame them, it would be directly to them, maybe with others or shaming them when I think about them, I harm not only them but yes, I harm myself. In the beginning was the word and every thought, even more when I'm awakening of the beliefs and convictions, works like a very strong spell. Words told to myself or others create the way I experience reality. If I become aware of it I have the chance to use words with the intention of love. If the intention while speaking to someone isn't love but shame and segregation it is then that I cursed not only the other but I cursed myself. I create an oath to myself where I say you cannot when you do not. There it is where I cage the other and myself. There it is where I don't allow others to heal therefore I don't allow myself to heal. I wound myself.

This is a practice to unpractise the belief of the unhealthiness of others to heal myself and learn that health, peace and freedom doesn't need to be impacted on any physiological condition. We may regenerate or degenerate, it's the perspective on both that shapes the experience. This is only one life: you can see it in a smaller scale as just one day; each day you feel different, the weather is never the same, one day hard, one day soft, sometimes forests burn, sometimes they flood, sometimes they bloom. That is what nature in all states has in common, it just is while doing what it is doing— nature just is.

This is a very short and efficient practice. Please take a pen and write down every person that comes into your mind that you shamed regarding health. Now take a thought of gratitude for each person where it was that this person inspired you to be more healthy. Send that gratitude to this person. To make it more efficient write for each person a few sentences and send it to them or tell them personally. From now on allow yourself to see that healing starts when you allow the other to heal.

# 18. The Future of Nutrition

When I say that I feel how food in my body communicates with the cells and alters their state and the way they reproduce, I mean it literally that way. From a scientific point of few it is nutrigenomics and nutrigenetics that impairs or supports general health. So when I choose food for me it is food that one could say supports my gene expression; intuition knows what science reveals. For me the future of nutrition is learning to communicate with what supports my 'cellular health' while keeping in mind that the concept of health shall be revealed by listening to the wisdom of intuition.

'Over time, the relationship between diet and health has aroused great interest, since nutrition can prevent and treat several diseases. It has been demonstrated that general recommendations on macronutrients and micronutrients do not affect to every individual in the same way because diet is an important environmental factor that interacts with genes. Thus, there is a growing necessity of improving a personalized nutrition to treat obesity and associated medical conditions, taking into account the interactions between diet, genes and health. Therefore, the knowledge of the interactions between the genome and nutrients at the molecular level, has led to the advent of nutritional genomics, which involves the sciences of nutrigenomics and nutrigenetics. *NCBI The future of nutrition: Nutrigenomics and nutrigenetics in obesity and cardiovascular diseases.* Peña-Romero AC1, Navas- Carrillo D2, Marín F3, Orenes-Piñero E1.

# 19. Cognitive Health

Does cognitive health have an influence on the way we understand our intuitive wisdom? Consumption of a so-called vast composition of macronutrients has a strong impact on the brain's function. I suggest that the clearer the body is from factors the less it may fall into unconscious patterns. I feel that the essence beyond it transcends physiology thus it is still a part while being a part of the third-dimensional reality. And yes, as it is above, so it is below. Paracelsus emphasised that there is nothing on this planet that is not in heaven. Depending on how many years we reside within the body the body may show signs of decay or not. Like my friend Anita would say, 'What we can't manage this life we will manage in the next one till we understood that there is something that manages effortlessly.'

If we nourish the physiology or here specifically the brain with nutrients that benefit our bodies health expression we change as well cognitive health. My suggestion here is that if my brain works well I may better understand how to interpret the wealth that my cellular wisdom offers. I start to understand 'mycellf'. Rapid brain ageing which occurs by a life that is not lived holistically, which includes malnutrition and stress, are then factors that may make it more complex to communicate with the inner guide.

The biological factor of brain ageing is impacted by the nutritional interventions. When learning to listen to the intuitive nutritional needs we may support the brain which expresses the intellectual understanding of the wisdom that we may get offered. Keep in mind that compulsive nutrition is a risk factor for the development of cognitive impairment and disorder. So the more years we spend here may be a greater factor for neurodegeneration. I want to mention that fasting, especially intermittent fasting, or caloric restriction have proven to be active supporters when it comes to treatments and delay of neuronal ageing, supporting an increase in the healthspan and delaying neurodegeneration. Plant-derived polyphenols and antioxidants, low animal protein intake and a plant-based diet improve lifespan when applied in a holistic and intuitive approach. If you want to actively support your brain with nature's gifts you may go to the health store and see where you feel drawn to or research which foods give neuronal support and then choose intuitively what works for you.

For me, it was spirulina. When I saw it first and felt my body drawn to it I started researching and found that it was used successfully by NASA as a nurturing supporter on space missions for astronauts. Besides the support that it provides in neuroprotection and its impact in cognitive functions, spirulina prevents memory dysfunction. Organic spirulina has anticancer, antiviral and antiallergic effects. It is an example of a nature-given food that does not need to be processed chemically, it already is perfect in its composition. Often it is thought that there is no connection to what we eat and how we feel and think or even general intelligence. But yes, there is, I feel it within all of my cells and science is here as a supporter to better understand why or how.

Another factor which science sees as important is a nutrition that is rich in algae omega-3 fatty acids as it is supporting in upregulating genes and cognitive processes so the brain works better which for me has the outcome of effortless and self-inspiring creativity and productivity. When it comes to the genetic part the support of algae omega-3 fatty acids is important for maintaining synaptic function and positive neuroplasticity. On the other hand, a nutrition which does not support the cells and is mostly rich in high animal derived foods, chronic stress, daily consumption of caffeine, which is significant in the increases of the amygdala activity and promotes those so-called amygdala hijacks, and saturated fats reduce the body's molecular substrates which work as helpers in the processing of cognitive functions. So what happens if we consume lots of those saturated fats? It is a factor that supports neurological dysfunction. Looking at the word dysfunction in Wikipedia which is described as: 'A failure to function in an expected or complete manner. Usually refers to a disorder in a bodily organ (e.g. erectile dysfunction), a mental disorder, or the improper behavior of a social group.' Which seems quietly accurate and it's understandable why the impact of food may interfere with our behaviour. So to underline that once again, food, yes, impacts the way we think, feel and behave.

'We now know that particular nutrients influence cognition by acting on molecular systems or cellular processes that are vital for maintaining cognitive function.'

'In addition to the capacity of the gut to directly stimulate molecular systems that are associated with synaptic plasticity and learning, several gut hormones or peptides, such as leptin, ghrelin, glucagon-like peptide 1 (GLP1) and insulin have been found to influence emotions and cognitive processes (FIG. 1).'

'Dietary manipulations are a viable strategy for enhancing cognitive abilities and protecting the brain from damage, promoting repair and counteracting the effects of aging.' *Brain foods: the effects of nutrients on brain function* by Fernando Gómez-Pinilla

So we see that the brain's function to work properly has various ways to be supported. Learning to listen how the body with all its senses and the mind reacts to food and how our cells respond supports greater awareness on the individual given holistic health. Know when it is that you are practising a belief and when you unpractise and have a real chat with your cells. This is a recurring practice that goes through this book; invite yourself into yourself and communicate with the wisdom the body has to offer. Productivity, creativity and a better brain function may be a great byproduct. Know if it is for the sake of living intuitively and following joy or the belief to achieve. No day is the same and finding the space beyond harming and healing, productive and unproductive, creative and uncreative is where the individual perfection awakens. We use this body as a tool to express our self while living on this planet. We may care for it or not, and the one who will have to handle it is the identifying self, the one who handles it will be effortless in the essence of doing so.

I give you every seed-bearing plant on
the face of the whole earth and every
tree that has fruit with seed in it.
They will be yours for food

—Bible

We are never more than one grateful thought
away from peace of heart

—Brother David Steindl-Rast

# 20. Ancestors, Genetics and Gratitude

Very often we hear that many reasons we are sick, not happy in life or relationships, from intimate to family, or can't live joyfully has its roots in our genes. Is that a fact? Actually we incarnate here not only with lots of information that our ancestors gave us but as well with the individual and collective beliefs. So how does epigenetics show us it is the behaviour rather than actually the genetic part that can increase mental or physiological conditions? The social and ethical behaviour leads us to a repetitive pattern that already our family members had. The external world can be a wonderful mirror to see one's reflection. It can be even just a small note like 'you are starting to be more and more like your parents'; this can be seen as a criticism or a compliment but here I want to invite you to not identify with the compliment or criticism but yes, to look at it neutrally. This helps you to understand your patterns and find your intuitive individuality rather than the family member's value patterns. We all will have traits from the ones that gifted us with life. This is a simple technique to integrate and divide what has been created through a growing up trauma and to understand when it is that I'm acting out of behaviour that was practised and is or isn't holistic. It will always be your choice what you choose. Just notice that a life that has integrated all is a life that is lived joyfully. It is my way. I can tell you with all of my heart that to notice the difference and then don't make a difference is the birth of peace. Nice when you are using your family or your lived experiences as a reason to not be able to live a joyful life. I invite you to look beyond beliefs and use the 10 Point Intuition Cell-Awareness Method.

Besides the 10 Point Intuition Cell-Awareness Method at least once a year I invite you to write a gratitude letter.

Take a pen and write a letter to your ancestors in gratitude to all that you are grateful for. There is always something to find what we are grateful for. Write a letter with an open heart, just write without stopping. Let it flow and fall into yourself how it is to be grateful. As you have noticed I love to connect the inner wisdom with the wisdom of science; here it is wonderful that it has been recognised that research studies in this field indicate that gratitude is associated with an enhanced sense of personal well-being. So why gratitude?

The root of joy is gratefulness... It is not joy that makes us grateful; it is gratitude that makes us joyful

—Brother David Steindl-Rast

In the morning I'm the morning, in noon I'm the noon, evening I turn into night and everyone has a different nuance. We can't be always the same; for the identity it might feel like destruction but there is no thing such as destruction, there is only transformation.

Okay, but then isn't living intuitively not a concept as well with the call on getting healthier? You got it. What is core here for me is that intuition has a piece of knowledge that's beyond concepts. If I look at it from clinical research and compare it with what I call intuition, which is always a joyful guide, it tells me that living from joy and combining biomedical research is the path for a human experience that can be more comfortable. But consider it may be that something in the laboratory or a clinical trial acts in a specific way being perceived through the eyes of the scientist. It as well is formed through the intention of how the outcome should be depending on whether it was sponsored by industry, government, academia, nonprofit organisations or other health advocates. The intention may be as well purposes of pre-explanation on how things are going to interact with the cellular behaviour or then placebo or nocebo. But here is the crucial part. Nothing ever happens again the same way it has happened in this 3-D experience.

So how to get more integrated with those thoughts of genetic health, personal health or the healthism trap? Next time you recognise yourself judging health beliefs about yourself or others, take a moment and invite yourself into yourself. I like to use here the breath and a moment to imagine how I am coming home into myself. I love the mind as a friend to connect to the essence and clear the filters of beliefs. I take five deep breaths and imagine myself flooding this body with my consciousness. Then it's possible to see how the cells start to glow. Now I re-evaluate if it was just conceptual that I would choose or if it as well would be my intuitive choice. The intuitive choice is mostly the one that first comes into mind after inviting myself to me again. If I should continuously choose scientifically unhealthy options, I can practise to understand the cellular wisdom with a intuitive reset method for improving general health.

Being guided by the intuition activates the natural given gift of compassion of your cells, being aware of your cells' needs, and empathy towards others and yourself which includes the understanding of what nourished them physiologically. Practising to reconnect to the intuition activates compassion that gives us courage to respond to suffering. It supports ourselves and others. Compassion is being interested and curious, like a child, to the experiences of every entity. It connects us with an effortless reactivity which comes out of the heart.

Compassion leads to greater well-being for oneself, and less stress in challenging social situations. Intuition is the initiator of compassion and shows us what's behind the scenes. It is the realisation of peace and freedom in every human. The ability to have compassion isn't about being weak or submissive to the given moment. For me it feels like gratitude to the other for sharing what the other feels like, gratitude for just being together without expectations as well; it is understanding the other and looking at the other with two eyes as reality is showing me. This gives us the ability to be connected and inspire to help, with that childlike essence of non-judgmental curiosity.

Intuition gifts us to learning, feeling and experiencing how this physical body works. Being intuitive allows us to embrace empathy, compassion, love and kindness— and here I want to mention what is crucial to understand—only if there is not the intention to do so. Thus they could be seen as skills, helping to evolve in a peaceful way and making the experience of being human a gentle one.

Our feelings, physical and emotional, provide us with valuable information about our connection to the intuition. Are we judgemental, negative, uncaring, unloving, sad, angry or even scared? How do my cells feel right now when I experience something that takes my freedom and peace away? Through this connection that intuition gives us we develop the ability to arrive in the present moment and see what is. It's non-practising, it's letting intuition flow without holding it back.

So now we know through living a holistic and intuitive life we become able to create awareness of the cellular wisdom and recognise emotions as a biochemical response in our body that can enhance or filter the intuition.

Intuition helps us to see reality. We can distinguish between what our personal convictions and values are and what it is that our inner wisdom wants to express. By engaging with reality and loving what is, we align with peace, health and freedom. It allows us to look behind the story our mind creates about us and others. It opens the opportunity to switch from the view of how our life is going to be or should and shouldn't be, to a vaster and more generous self-caring way. We utilise this gift to become more conscious of what is real and what is imagined.

Once we have engaged with reality and seen what's behind what we are feeling, we realise the convictions of why we're feeling it. Through living intuitively we gain this huge opportunity to easier understand the egoic identity patterns and to experience and understand the emotions and feelings of others.

Earth is a wonderful ground to flourish, integrate and sustain intuition which is the portal to peace, health and freedom. All that comes from our intuition can help us effectively to manage life full of empathy and compassion. Please not that speaking about those qualities is a pointer to use language but the essence of it can be in my actual perspective only experienced. We are gifted with the courage to engage into suffering and be of caring and loving service to all residing beings of earth.

I really invite you from all of my heart to live and spread the wisdom of how to live intuitively with everyone. So we all can recall that intuition wants the best for everyone, that is why it creates the platform of world peace without having the need of creating it. It always seeks universal harmony and peace.

To study the way is to study the self. To study the self is to forget the self. To forget the self is to be enlightened by all things. To be enlightened by all things is to remove the barriers between one's self and others

—Dogen

# 21. Is Intuition Convincing?

How to distinguish convictions and intuition. How can you question what is a concept and what comes from your intuition? You will actually just know it and feel it once you have inherited the 10 Point Intuition Cell-Awareness Method. From there, go far beyond beliefs of how intuition should be, we can reach the intuition through our convictions. Let's gets more aware on actual food choices.

Let's say I am going to the supermarket and my body draws me to the carrot section with lots of different carrots, like black, purple, orange and white ones. I take the orange carrots as I feel immediately drawn to them. I feel my body pendulate, reaching out to the orange carrots. Then I take a look to the right and I see purple carrots. I remember that I read an article that purple carrots are so much more healthy than the orange ones that I've chosen intuitively. So I actually don't really feel drawn to them but I buy them because of the concept that I have about health. Can you see the pattern that happened to me here? Instead of listening to my intuition I listened to the convictions of my mind. I'm a huge fan of biomedical research that includes nutritional science as well. But our body has such a wonderful gift of knowing naturally what's good.

So what do carrots have to do with peace, freedom, wisdom or health? Well, the body itself that is the portal to the intuition is the vehicle with which we experience life. So by not listening to the intuition and choosing concepts we do not allow ourselves to have free choices; we choose because of concepts, that is the opposite of freedom. We leave the opportunity behind to give ourselves nourishment that was asked through the intuitive wisdom of the body. We listen to the thought that purple carrots are more healthy and get away from the possibility to have a healthy life because maybe what the body asked for in the first place is exactly what is needed. If the body is not aligned the mind is in trouble. If the mind is not aligned the body is in trouble.

Why did I choose food as an example here? Because that is what we are constantly caring about and reflecting on. It is something easy to apply in the day-by-day life. This leads to not practising and just trusting intuition. Remember that nature was created without machines and the intuitive wisdom of nature and its ways to get nourished can be filtered through the microbiome and the beliefs of nourishment.

Any practice in this book is a tool that I wrote with the intention to unpractise the practice of believing and open the space for all that is beyond beliefs, convictions and certainties. All the practices here will deepen the experience of connection between self and others. A deeper state of intuitive and intellectual relationship to distinguish the egoic identity-focused needs from the intuitive ones. When I allow myself to give up my beliefs and let presence flow I transcend my convictions and biases and become aware of them. Connecting to what exists creates the ability to live peacefully while staying on this beautiful planet.

The following imagination practice will clear old beliefs and open perspectives. It works best if you record it and listen to it from your own voice or with the help of another person that can guide you through this meditation. After a few times you probably will be able to practise it without external guidance, just with yourself as the guide and the traveller. This meditation will connect you to your intuition and create a state of 'cellfulness', so being aware what the cells need and inviting yourself into your cells. After this meditation you will find a couple of questions for you to answer. If you feel like it, you can also do the questions before and after. This imagination practice arose in the moment that I experienced my new birth, a gift that I received from this new birth experience. Allow yourself to go into this meditation without the effort to have an outcome. Just experience it and see what it feels like.

Lay in a comfortable position.

Do a body scan from feet to head.

Feel your inner body with all its organs. Feel your skin, your teeth, your bones and your hair.

Feel the blood within you flowing through all the body.

Take a moment to give attention on all at once.

Now expand your attention. Keep attention on your whole body and expand it, feel the floor that you are lying on.

Expand your attention to be your body and be the floor in the same time.

Keep attention on the whole body, be the floor and the earth under you.

Now go into the earth to the center of planet Earth. Expand your attention, be present in your body and in the earth.

Now expand it to be all continents. Feel how it is to be Earth.

Now expand it even further, keep attention as well in the body, expand it to be the air. Feel how it is to be the air. Feel the clouds.

Expand it more, be the trees and plants. Be the water.

Be the light. Keep attention in your body and be all humans and animals. Feel how it is connected to everything.

Expand it and become the houses, cars, music, become the sounds.

Now be the whole planet. Go further expand your energy to be the space and the planet. Become all planets, stars and suns.

Keep attention on everything that is in this universe.

Now expand it even further and imagine you are opening the physical dimension to access what's behind it. Expand to be the network that flows through all physical objects. The network that is the construction plan of all beings. Now expand it even further and be the source where it is coming from. Open the dimension that's behind infinity. Go to the source of existence. Be the source of existence. Be all and be nothing.

Feel how it is to be interconnected with all that is.

Now answer me this question:

Who are you?

Who are you?

Who are you?

Now take your time

feel

and I leave it open for you to stay longer in this state to experience it. Stay as long as you feel to.

Recognise now after you come back to this very moment with open eyes how you're feeling right now.

Questions for you to answer after or before and after:

**Are you remembering your name right now?**

**Are you focusing on changing your emotional state right now?**

**Are you focusing on remembering or changing what was yesterday or imagining what's going to happen tomorrow?**

**Are you judgemental and have the urge to do or change anything or anybody right now? (can relate to people, finances, the way life goes, your emotional state or this very moment)**

Let every answer sink in for a couple of minutes. To come to an end now, a last question.

**Do you feel like you need anything in this very moment?**

I invite you with all of my heart to share living from the intuition with others. This invitation for you to share how to live intuitively is the gateway to a world in peace.

In the last few years I developed different practices to deepen intuitive knowledge. Do I think they are very important? I don't know what they are but I sense what they do. There has not been one person I met that wasn't woven into a deeper sense of connection. I learned that the wisdom that I live from my intuition is created through the intellectual mind and a practice that isn't practising.

It is not easy to speak on an outcome that intuition has as it can create the need to have one. Let me ask you just to have a short intellectual break to invite yourself, just for a moment, into yourself. Notice the words with your two eyes and open your heart as often as you remember as it is the portal to intuition. The practices in this book can be like the realisation of oneself and the other without having a past or future. For me intuition demonstrates that there is no such thing as a truly existing story that has to manage the way one sees oneself or others. Through connecting with all that is, through connection to the intuition, we clear all convictions and it allows us to see things not only as they appear in our mind. We gain reality back and can see what really is in front of our two eyes and all that's behind it. Objects and entities in their wholeness and not limited to their stories and experiences. Of those practices, one is the arrival in the moment.

Looking with the two eyes deepens the understanding of the intuitive individual self as coherent thus always in impermanence. It's the opportunity to be in a way non-attached to what was and what hasn't happened yet. So we release our convictions and gain the freedom of non-conceptual reality. If we live from our intuition we will be aware what fills our mind and what fills our heart as both are qualities for the human experience on this planet. If I benefit can even be an initiation; if we flow with intuition there is no need to benefit as it already is within the whole intuition package. Intuition is like all-inclusive. It is transformation of subconscious, unconscious and conscious into the wisdom beyond those three.

As you know already biomedical research plays a key role in determining intellectually how the physiology in general works. Look how science underlines the importance of arriving in the moment, utilising the tool of attention and what role meditation plays. Please consider that even reading this individuality of each intuitive way of living should still be included.

We are not victims of aging, sickness and death. These are part of scenery, not the seer, who is immune to any form of change. This seer is the spirit, the expression of eternal being

—Deepak Chopra

The concept of being the creator of reality as a segregative entity takes away the power of real freedom. Too often we lose the beauty of being human by an egoic belief that there is nothing to be needed from the external world, that can be from advice, to a relationship, to social or work connections ... it can even be the avoidance of the external world because the conceptual mind loves to see oneself as the only opportunity to have peace alone. What I have learned is that whenever there is segregation, not from the intention of peace or curiosity, but yes, with the aim of disconnection, there occurs fragmentation. What does that mean? That we include in our lives a cage which brings us apart from the freedom of living the human experience. Whenever I think I create peace on my own and whenever a circumstance is coming in my path that isn't peace and I push it away that leads to an unbalanced life.

Let's say someone is sure that peace comes from within and believes that the external world is the one that creates all kind of fights, wars, arguments etc. Okay, this attitude can feel good for a while when I go in a wood cabin for several days or even live there, but what if I take that thought into my relationship with my partner, parents, closest friends or even my children? What happens when I think that my child is taking my peace away and I can have only peace on my own? Too often our beliefs damage not only our physiology and psychological experience but yes, the ones from those who stay closest to us. Believing that we only can have peace when we make others do what we think they should do, that's not freedom, that's not peace, that's not love.

So what is it in my relationships that creates love, freedom and peace? It is when I listen with an open heart as far as I can to understand, to not only understand the other but to mirror it and see where it is that I'm led by the mind rather than my intuition. Every human is individual and I know that each person's intuition if schooled knows how to create those three: we could even call them virtues, peace, freedom and love. None of those mean you have to accept everything or not accept. Intuition leads you to interact in any relationship with a harmonious interested exchange of individuality. Any relationship issue grows with the idea that the counterpart is not understanding one's perspective and/ or wanting the other to adopt one's perspective with the intention of proving them wrong. If the intention of an 'officially' solution-oriented conversation is not peace or curiosity it's an opportunity to unfilter inner beliefs.

To understand what filters are we need to look at social and ethical values which are guidelines on cultural grounds, telling us what is okay to do and what isn't. We inherit those beliefs from religion, our family, social groups, ethical settings and other cultural settings. Which guidelines or values we have depends on what is allowed or acceptable or what isn't. When we are born we are born with the opportunity to express ourselves individually by our incarnated consciousness and what we were gifted from our ancestors, which includes all joyful and all traumatic experiences. To live a holistic life we can learn to integrate all those parts. Learn what works best to express this physiological manifestation in its vastness to connect intellectually towards oneself and others. We are not disconnected from a deeper dimension seen but we can still intellectually feel disconnected which is the root of every emotional condition and secretive thought which leads to violations and crimes from psychological to physiological in relation to living beings or objects.

## Practice For Relationship Obstacles

Here is a practice for relationship obstacles.

You will need a pen and a paper or your notebook.

This is a practice to unpractise beliefs.

Find a place where you feel comfortable.

To start take a few moments to arrive within you.

Invite yourself into yourself through the breath.

Feel how your consciousness is flowing through all of your body, imagine all cells, even the space between the cells is given your full attention.

Now answer the following questions; this is an intense journalling exercise, take your time to do it completely. Some questions may sound abstract so let yourself experience the answers rather than trying to find an intellectual question.

Is there a living being, a place or an object that you feel disconnected from and not understood by in the last days?

Just sense and feel who and what the situation was.

Now allow yourself to go into the perspective of the living being, the place or object and feel into it how it feels to be in the other's shoes.

Let the feelings emerge, it doesn't matter how abstract the answer may sound. As soon as you recognise your mind wandering and thoughts arising let yourself arrive again and come back to the question.

How would I feel if I were the living being, the place or object that I feel disconnected from?

Let the answer emerge from within. Trust your inner visions and allow yourself to be the other rather than trying to explain how the other would feel.

Ask yourself again.

How would I feel if I were the living being, the place or object that I feel disconnected from?

Let the answer be your guide.

There is a force within that gives you life
Seek that.
In your body there lies a priceless jewel
Seek that.
Oh wanderer
If you are in Search of the greatest treasure,
don't look outside,
Look within, and seek That

—Rumi.

# 22. Body Pendulum

Intuition is about moving from compulsion to intuitive choice. Intuition does not avoid, deny, suppress any negative or positive feelings or emotions. It's the integration of all parts of the self. It supports us to have compassion and empathy towards the own convictions. Living through the intuition allows to love what is and always to express our inner truth with curiosity and kindness. This gifts us with an alternative to the always hungry egoic identity that often loves to fights with what is and nourishes itself simply from pleasant and unpleasant emotions. It can become a great suppressor of unpleasant emotions.

If we do not listen to what we are feeling we won't be able to see the truth that reality wants to mirror for us. Unpleasant emotions that are not ignored are like a guideline to recognise if I'm connected to my intuition in this very moment. Non-judgement that arises through intuition is a wonderful way of living from the heart. It is the only way to live in peace, freedom of mind and serendipity. If we live intuitively we will train to live without judgements that harm our cells and this form of existence will lead to an overall wellbeing and inspiration to experience life as it comes.

We are all considered social beings with a gifted ability for social cognition. Intuition increases this ability to understand others' emotions, convictions, intentions and beliefs.

Where is my dwelling place? Where I can never stand. Where is my final goal, toward which I should ascend?

It is beyond all place. What should my quest then be? I must, transcending God, into the desert flee

— Roger Housden

For Lovers of God Everywhere: Poems of the Christian Mystics (2009); p. 78.

We all have a genetic given intuition that helps us to recognise what is healthy for our physical and emotional expression. Going further from consumption to connection and imagination practices we can use this given gift of intuition to clear old beliefs and have the ability to choose what benefits us and lets us live holistically. Consumption of food is a wonderful topic here which will from time to time reappear in this book. Our beliefs cage us often in strong guidelines and validations for every theory of how we should eat and live. Diets or dogmatic food choices are only temporary and if adapted from somebody else not intuitive. So how are we even supposed to navigate our way through all of these convictions? Is there even a right answer that's coming from someone else on how I should eat, drink, live or behave?

What I got from my new birth experience was the ability to learn how to live intuitively and that each of us is special and individual in that expression. What might be good for you can be another person's poison. What is wonderful here is that as soon as we connect to our intuition we can lead others to their individual way of living intuitively effortlessly. Why effortlessly? When you inherit the presence of intuition within all your cells it will shine through your physiology and you cannot not teach it. Every being will be affected by it.

I love practical examples as well and our body communicates on such a deep wisdom with the external world that he knows effortlessly what is needed to nurture when living intuitively. For example, who can we trust when we are navigating our way through the supermarket? It really is not just diets and lifestyle changes that are leading us away from intuition. It is the variation of fresh and processed foods that lead the mind to intellectualise or emotional forms of choices that come from learned patterns. Labels, pictures, benefits and reviews lead us to believe other beliefs or others' intuition choices.

## How do we apply this in the supermarket?

**Stand, calm your mind, become still as best as you can within your environment.**

If it is easier for you, you can close your eyes and ask your body to show you a yes. Stay calm and still and you will feel your body move in a particular direction.

Now take a breath, center and ask your body to show you a no. Be aware in which direction your body is leading you.

What's an example of how to apply it somewhere else, if you're at home going to your fruit basket and cannot distinguish if it is the mind telling you what you would need to nourish the physical body? Here is an easy way to learn what the body wants. Take two different fruits, let's say strawberries and blueberries, and then hold each in the hand alone. So in my case moving to the front is a yes and moving backwards is a no. Ask yourself, do you want to be nourished from these blueberries? If your body moves softly to the front you can now take the strawberries and ask the same; if you do not move or move to the back you can be sure that your body is asking for the strawberries. This is just a super simple application to do in moments that we do not feel connected or are not travelling in our beliefs. You can turn this around as well. Notice that your real intuition is non-judgemental; it will even when your body turns to the back not judge the fruit as bad or not good for you right now, it's just a neutral and gentle, no thank you!


Even if this is a very conceptual way of accessing the intuition it is a great way to train conceptually what is not intuition. Only when i know what it is not it seems that i can know what it is.

God is an utter Nothingness,
Beyond the touch of Time and Place:
The more thou graspest after Him,
The more he fleeth thy embrace

—The Cherubinic Wanderer
Translation by J. E. Crawford Flitch (1932)

# 23. Holistic Body/Mind Connection

Apart from what your intuition is telling you, what does science advocate for a healthy body/mind experience? Before I elaborate here, I often get asked how it happened that I got so interested in what science reveals. As I mentioned in this book, science for me is the intellectual understanding of how the physiology in the three-dimensional world works. I would love you just to explore how science works for you and see if your intuition finds its individual ground principle for holistic health as well. The researchers from Harvard Medical School identified six steps which can promote general health.

**Step 1:** Eat a plant-based diet

**Step 2:** Exercise regularly

**Step 3:** Get enough sleep

**Step 4:** Manage your stress

**Step 5:** Nurture social contacts

**Step 6:** Continue to challenge your brain

Even if this information is valuable for a physically healthy body, keep in mind that a state of peace and freedom of mind is not dependent on any lifestyle change. Your intuition is the best guide to help you find your own way. This information is just a guideline to combine the physical and the metaphysical, as we are here to experience both. I think they can be good guidelines. Thus, if I live them just as a concept they may turn into belief systems.

What is probably the best way to eat? A plant-based diet?

Take a moment and let that sink in.

Is a plant-based diet the best way to eat?


Yes, you got it. The best way to eat and live is your individual and intuitive way. We can always consider the beautiful science that can help us better understand how the body works in the 3D identified way. There is much more than only three dimensions. Have you recognised how a belief can shape the way we perceive things and filters to see the opportunity to live intuitively? Your body knows what is best for you. Always.


Consumption of any kind alters the way our microbiome responds. There is wonderful new science in genomic medicine which studies the health/ condition process based on the interaction of the human genes with the environment.

Did you know that instincts that we have, emotions that we experience and behaviour that we express are all biological processes? They work in an interconnected plan to support us in survival. The human race is in constant evolution and as well a result of evolutionary processes. Psychological and physiological nourishment is needed for this three dimension. We have intuitive triggers that are led by our instincts of survival. We have each day a different demand on energy and our instinctive intuitive behaviour supports us well when we are aware of what is coming from the call of the deeper wisdom. As our consumption behaviour changes we as well interact with vaster genetic variations. When it comes to food I have noticed that especially refined foods filter the body's intuitive nourishment wisdom. Interestingly mostly highly processed foods support a gut dysbiosis which activates the body's inflammation mode. Can you recall the inflammation in negative thinking and depression? Those are key factors which can lead to chronic conditions as well.

What does this mean? Food, and all kinds of information, interact with the microbiome in our gut, and this may sound funny, but the microbiome is able to interact with our choices, missing the opportunity to live intuitively, resulting in a case of misunderstood food choices leading to inflammation. Inflammation from a holistic view is rather living from concepts than living from within, not enjoying the self, dislike of the proper body image, dislike of caring for ones physiology, dislike of the life situation, and many more other stressful belief patterns that make the physical and emotional body suffer. It is being inflamed mentally and physiologically. This is as well a concept and it might be a beautiful romanticism and it as well can cage one in an identification of a condition or be a pointer to where I can deepen my intuitive knowledge. Here it is important to not judge the inflammation as bad; it's just a sign in the body that something is not aligned the way the physical body would prefer to have it.

"Whoever said the small things don't matter has never seen a match start a wildfire."

—Beau Taplin

Let me tell you about an experience I had a little while ago. I had been giving a lecture on how to live healthier by living holistically. The main topic this day was the connections from physiology to psychology regarding food ingestion. The question came up how to live healthy in an environment that is full of toxicity, leftovers of medications, radiation in the drinking water and pesticides. So the big question around this topic was how is it even possible to live healthy here on this planet with so many environmental factors. For that let's practise and see what intuition would tell us. I will leave the answers open, so just go into the questions and see if the answers open your cells or if they get closed. Trust your intuition, as it always and in any given moment wants you to feel the joy that life has to offer. I would like you to imagine that all those environmental factors have an impact on your health. Feel into it, how does it feel to think about it? What are your thoughts and emotions arising, making yourself aware? This is an imagining exercise. Use the beautiful tool that the mind offers. Imagination. Now please use one environmental factor that you feel is impacting you. For example ...
*The food doesn't have more nutrients because monoculture or pesticides are making us all sick ...*


After this 10 Point Intuition Cell-Awareness Method practice I will give you some reflection points. You will see similarities to the other 10 Point methods practices in this book. The aim is to find different ways of connecting to the inner believes by different wordings and learn to identify, integrate and metabolize the

194

informations that the cells offer. The 10 Point Intuition Cell-Awareness Method is a flexible technique which always schools the intuitive guidance skills and supports in transforming and metabolizing past experiences to use them as a source of wisdom.

**1. Do you have the feeling that something was or is strange, inconsistent or not right? Please describe it.**

**2. Write one to three advices from you to the person or moment on how it should be, act, behave or interact regarding statement 1.**

**3. Do you trust that intuition guides you to a life in joy?**

**4. Please describe the feelings and thoughts you have about the statement in question 1. How do you feel?**

**5. Does the feeling of statement 3 bring you health, freedom, joy or peace?**

**6. Now go back to the moment of the statement from question 1.**

**Do you think that your intuition was to let you receive the information from question 1. knowing**

that your intuition wants you to live healthy, free and in joy and peace?

7. What happens to you, how do you respond to yourself and/or your counterpart if you trust the statement from point 1?

8. What would happen to your behaviour towards yourself, others and this particular moment if you were guided by your intuition?

9. In addition to the notes from 8, please specify exactly the moments in which the contrary statement took place or is taking place.

10. Now refer to statement 1. Use this as a mirroring practice. So relate it to you, contrary to others and contrary to the moment that you described. Then go to statement 2, use it as a mirror for you, a mirror to the perspective of others and find ways of turning it around.

As you finish this practice I would like you to let the answers really sink in and look again when it is that you feel that your cells are opening up or when they are closing. They listen all the time. This practice is very powerful to recognise the power of the mind. It's the power of creation or destruction of oneself.

Too often we choose out of compulsion and not an intuitive choice which goes from choices of emotional consumption to physiological. It is not only our beliefs but as you know as well the microbiome that controls food cravings. If I allow myself to practise the behaviour of my microbiome just by taking three days of choosing scientifically proven beneficial foods within the intuitive approach I start already to change the behaviour and symbiosis of the microbiome. Three days are enough to make your microbiome change the signals sent to the brain and back. Another option i love is to get to 'zero consumption' with an intestinal cleanse and the following fasting to boost autophagy. It is essential to cleanse leftovers and substances that are stuck in the intercellular and intracellular space to reset the body's intuitive knowledge of health and metabolise cellular trash and damaged proteins and organelles. It is cellular cleansing by fasting. Fasting metabolises all leftovers from what we digest physically and it metabolises what we digest emotionally. It has the power to enhance the cleansing of cellular trauma holistically.

# 24. Fasting

A good way to cleanse the intuitive system and set it up for an upgrade is fasting.

The concept of fasting is neither new nor a form of dieting. It is practised in many religions for mental purification and cleansing of the soul. Moreover, it has positive effects on the body and the psyche and supports the detoxification and maintenance of our cells. A lasting change in our eating rhythms leads to rest in our digestive system. This rest subsequently transfers to the mind and we can return to our lives with increased awareness of what our cells need and expanded consciousness. Clear body, clear mind.

This can be a guideline but always keep in mind that each body is individual. True health is not related to any practice, physical condition or emotional identification. It is stopping to listen only to your intellect and explore what the intuition has to reveal. Considering what our experiences reveal as well as what studies provide can help us understand why our beliefs shape our life. But more important for each of us is to find an individual expression of health. Fasting clears all senses and resets them. The inner voice, what we call intuition, will be able to lead us to live a holistic life in peace and freedom.

With this in mind, I would love you to really see that emotions are always a good guideline to where health is leading us. The body is able to release not only toxins from the intercellular space but it also clears what could be called the 'cellular storage of traumata' and helps to release what was stuck from the past. Cells remember, and if we give them the chance to metabolise the information our body is getting all the time, we support them. Hippocrates, the father of medicine, is quoted as saying, 'bad digestion is the root of all evil' and 'death sits in the bowels'. What Hippocrates likely meant was that the gastrointestinal tract, or 'gut', is responsible for much more than digesting food; it plays a vital role in creating and sustaining physical and mental health.

Fasting supports our microbiome and therefore indirectly our immune system by protecting the body from parasitic germs. Several parasitic germs can interfere with our natural given intuitive responses by sending signals that give impulses so that we behave in ways that promote the reproduction of those parasitic germs. So you could see the vitalising practice of fasting as a time to clean up. You give your fabulous body the opportunity to relax a bit from all the work that it has done all these years. Often we just want to relax the mind and forget that the body as well is constantly working. If the mind has the right to relax, why not the body?

After a fast the body will be reset and full of energy. If we consider the body as a vehicle that expresses the state of the mind, then for optimal health it's important to eat more foods that give us life—made, prepared or cooked from our core, from our intuition. Food that's made to give love. If we clean our physical vehicle and then nourish it with life-giving, fresh foods we naturally detox from all old patterns.

So fasting activates the metabolisation of old stored knowledge and helps heal the physical and emotional body. How did I first fast? For every year of sin I fasted one day. Each day will take away one year of sin. What do I mean by sin? Several moments in time where I haven't been connected to my intuition. So, for example, if I would fast with, let's exaggerate a little and say 111 years, I would fast 111 days. Maybe not at once but include per week a day or two. Sometimes I would do a couple of days where I would fast to reset my body. Like Hippocrates would have suggested how to keep the physical body in shape: 'He who wants to remain strong, healthy and young should take everything in moderation, exercise the body, breathe clean air and heal his hurts through fasting rather than medication.'

While looking deeper into the topic fasting with my friend the biologist Anita- Juliane Winkler Green we found that intermittent fasting was shown to improve cognitive function, brain structure and neuroplasticity, which may help the brain to learn more easily. It's actually not only what you eat but also when you eat and how much you eat. Fasting as a vital and simultaneously life-prolonging process can no longer take place as soon as food intake occurs, because that results in a switch to energy recovery and leaves no time for the body's own repair mode. Fasting cleans up cellular waste and triggers an important process: autophagy (self-digestion). The Japanese cell biologist Yoshinori Ohsumi received a Nobel Prize for the discovery of this endogenous recycling system within the body. Damaged organelles, like mitochondria (the powerhouses of the cell), and misfolded proteins, are thereby broken down independently. Further studies confirmed that autophagy can counteract degenerative illnesses like Alzheimer's, cancer and cardiovascular conditions. That was especially interesting for us because we both remember in times we have been sick we did not want to eat anything. So as a child our caring parents wanted us to feel better by eating something. 'You need to eat, darling, to get better' but our bodies did not feel like it. So it makes a lot of sense for us to trust the intuitive wisdom.

# 25. Fasting Changes the Reality We Perceive in the World

So, let us have a look at the connection of food deprivation neuroplasticity. Neuroplasticity seen as the neuroscientific name given to a phenomenon that demonstrates what we do, think and pay attention to changes our brain. Structural and functional and yes, even in adults. The intermittent fasting which I would do when I consume food within the 24 hour period in the window of 1-6 hours makes me feel more productive, creative, more vital. That happens because while fasting the liver glycogen stores are depleted and then ketones are produced from fat cells. The amazing thing is that, yes, it doesn't make the body feel better but it interacts with the molecular and cellular adaptations of our neuronal networks in the brain which boosts the resilience, resistance to stress, injuries and illness. Fasting utilised in a holistic way is a powerful tool. So it doesn't need to be a long period of fasting but a period of a minimum of 16 hours optimises the brain function, especially the ones involved in cognition and mood. It's like a training of 16 hours; I train my metabolism to recycle and eight hours I train my metabolism to absorb better. This kind of metabolic switching impacts the pathways where the signals are sent, therefore promoting neuroplasticity.

Generally fasting and exercising protects neurons against stress and helps the mitochondrial biogenesis and cell growth while for example recovering from exercise. Metabolising past experiences is one thing I feel in fasting as a powerful healing method of trauma. Digestion is seen as an exercise here as well. So fasting is the thing, yes.

> *"Fasting and exercise upregulate neurotrophic factor signalling, antioxidant and DNA repair enzymes, protein deacetylases and autophagy, which protects neurons against stress and sets the stage for mitochondrial biogenesis and cell growth and plasticity during recovery periods Lifestyles characterised by little or no IMS (three meals per day plus snacks and negligible exercise) result in suboptimal brain functionality and increase the risk of major neurodegenerative and psychiatric disorders. Many different IMS regimens are likely to improve brain health such that individuals may choose an approach that suits their particular daily and weekly schedules."* —Excerpt from Pubmed Intermittent metabolic switching, neuroplasticity and brain health; Mark P. Mattson, Keelin Moehl,

Nathaniel Ghena, Maggie Schmaedick & Aiwu
Cheng

What does that tell us? That the physical experience of
being human can be immensely changed not only by
changing our convictions and beliefs and clearing those
filters but yes, with a lifestyle change that changes the
physiological responses created through food ingestion
or less food ingestion (fasting or intermittent fasting).
Remember that here as well the type of food can from a
scientific view be the reason for more degeneration or
inflammation or more regeneration and antioxidative
activity.

Fasting supports it in a beautiful way. It is like giving the
body less of the constant information flow that it already
receives. When I started my first fasting I experienced
what it is to sense how the body feels without all the
information received from food. I started to digest music
differently, conversations in a totally new perspective,
and I could sense deeper how all beautifully interacts
with the body in a way that I didn't even have on my
radar. I felt neuroplasticity changing in a new, unknown
way.

Our nervous system, actually everything in our body, is
constantly evolving. Forming new memories is a way to
learn new things. Whether we identify with what we
experienced is yet a choice. The understanding in
neurobiology on how this happens is constantly gaining
new perspectives. What is known is, there are changes in

synapses and/or other parts of neurons that affect how information is processed and transmitted in the nervous system.

Neuroplasticity can go in both directions: the strength of information flowing through parts of the nervous system can increase (potentiation) or decrease (depression).

Neuroplasticity can happen at the synapse (synaptic neuroplasticity), or on the level of entire cells or total numbers of synapses where the target cell is changed (structural neuroplasticity). Let me elaborate a little bit more on neuroplasticity and the connection to meditation, empathy and what it has to do with general health.

Intuition as you know now itself can be just covered by our beliefs as well as have a physiological expression which is in the material world correlated to neuroplasticity. Often we think that some beliefs and convictions that we have or even the way that we react in life is not changeable because of an experience or trauma that we or our ancestors have lived. So often we think we can't change the way we are wired we have to live with it. Let me tell you here with all of my heart. In the beginning was the word and what you say and believe will immensely interact with what you experience in the material world. Because of that I love science as it always backs me up with all experiences that I ever had. It's not only what I have learned but yes, science shows that throughout a person's life, the brain has the ability to change. The brain's ability to readjust itself by creating new connections of neurons like we have learned is the so referred neuroplasticity.

A couple of years ago it was still thought that adults were not able to readjust their neuroplasticity and now we know better. Yes, we can rewire the brain and change its activity. An activity of the brain that is linked to a particular region can be transferred to an alternative location; there could also be a change in synapse strength or the proportion of the grey matter. Remember that during neuroplasticity there could be synaptic depression or synaptic potentiation? Synaptic depression occurs when there is reduced synaptic activity thus leading to a reduction in the neurotransmitters, receptors so the target cells have reduced response. In synaptic potentiation, there is increased synaptic activity due to increased release of neurotransmitters and increased response of target cells characterised by an increase in second messengers.

Something else that i found was that mindfulness meditation, which for me is 'cellfulness' and integrative body-mind training with relaxation training induces changes in specific brain networks and changes in brain state. It is not only science that reveals that this produces a molecular cascade which improves brain connectivity, otherwise called neuroplasticity. That is what I sense, see and feel when people do the self-invitation into onecellf. So sometimes things that we think are hardwired are not so hardwired and can be tuned differently, depending on our intention.

I want to mention as well that there have been many researches done in positive neuroplasticity changes which show the importance of how the practice of meditation or mindfulness relates to general health, there are evidence-based interventions like mindfulness meditation to have a positive direction in neuroplasticity which supports meditations having the potential to improve general health and 'slow the rate of cellular ageing'. For me mindfulness is inviting myself into 'mycellf'.

Too often we get into the self-defence mode where we try to defend our traumas. We can decide when it's time to let go and let the past, the present and the future evolve. We decide when we release the others from the cage we lock them which only exists in the past and in the imagination. Remember, it's always the egoic mind that doesn't want to be free and doesn't want to let the other be something different than the other was in the past. It's your choice to whom you listen. Listen to freedom or listen to a life that is caged in the past. My personal experience shows me daily, not only with me but with every person I meet, that if I allow myself and others to be free in every moment that my mind can capture I will experience freedom and peace. This goes into 'mycellf' then the unlocked past experiences get metabolised and the 'cellf' is evolving in a way that has a different quality of freedom. Besides what I experience it is science that treats me like a friend to back up what I have seen. Intuition is always right and even more if it sounds hurtful. I love science as it is the intellectual wisdom of intuition which in times where we haven't experienced freedom, there it is, where science can show me what beautiful opportunities I have while living on this planet.

Nerve cells particularly benefit from food deprivation, because they contain the largest number of mitochondria. The dysfunctional substances are contained within a membrane and transported to the lysosomes, which contain digestive enzymes. This way, protein parts are broken down into single amino acids that are used for the construction of new proteins. So the body reuses and metabolises what is not needed immediately. Isn't that amazing? Autophagy and ketosis also explain some physical functions of the well-known techniques of breatharianism and prana-consumption. Here, looking on a larger scale, quantum biology shows that those techniques allow the body to obtain its energy through metabolism of proteins and enhances the body's nutrient synthesis without food consumption. It intensifies the ability to metabolise information.

The processes of cellular cleansing and this renewal optimally supports the natural self-healing ability, enhances productivity, increases creativity and helps to release stored trauma

—Biologist Anita Juliane Winkler-Green

I always like to invite myself to see the intention to fast. Fasting improves symptoms of neurodegenerative conditions like multiple sclerosis. A ketogenic diet (80% fat and hardly any carbohydrates) mimics the effects of fasting and helps patients to relieve symptoms significantly outside of full fasting days as well. A ketogenic diet naturally stimulates feelings of satiety. Like during fasting, the brain obtains energy in the form of ketone bodies instead of sugars. Ketone bodies have another advantage over sugars: mitochondria are damaged in dementia as well as in cancer patients and are no longer able to function at full capacity. Correspondingly, they produce many free radicals. By contrast, ketone bodies promote formation of new mitochondria and improve the function of existing ones.

Fasting also affects gene expression and leads to functional changes in genes related to longevity and resistance against conditions. When we stop to ingest we have time to rest and digest. Not only food but as well all our beliefs, experiences and metabolic leftovers. Fasting causes increased amounts of the p53 protein in the liver. This protein is required to adapt the metabolism to fasting and is one of the main factors controlling cell growth. The p53 protein has the ability to interrupt the cell cycle and to prevent division of out-of-control cells. And the funny thing is that the liver itself in holistic medicine is seen as supporting the ability to focus. We often have felt that the energy that we would need to digest and to 'fight to get the food out' again was in moments where we have been eating only because of habit. This could be as well why fasting can be a crucial therapy option for metabolic conditions and cancer, having more energy left to resistance.

Did you ever have that moment where you have been super hungry all day long but didn't have a moment to eat and when you started to get your first meal there was not a lot of hunger left? In a hungry state, cell membranes are particularly open to resorption of high-quality nutrients and the cells can then make optimal use of them. Besides that the body as well finds a way to digest its leftovers from the work that was done.

You remember the second step at the Harvard medical school advice was exercise regularly. So here what was found is that intermittent fasting (fasting 16h +o-) seems to be optimised with sports. A training session of just 10 minutes already promotes oxygenation (oxygen saturation) of our blood and refreshes our entire being. Weight and endurance training can increase the intensity of fasting because they lead to higher caloric consumption. The body's own detoxification via self-metabolism of protein residues can be used as supporting treatment to help improve its inherent healing powers in case of elimination therapies, cleansing in case of yeast infections (candida), rehabilitation, as well as preventative and aftercare therapies such as chemotherapy. It's a great tool to communicate first with an physician.

So intermittent fasting not only helps with the metabolisation of excess weight, which often is an indicator for later risk of illness, but can also prevent conditions like diabetes and other metabolic disorders. Fasting rebalances our metabolism and we can switch between sugar and fat metabolism more easily. Furthermore, fewer toxins accumulate in the liver and insulin can be processed better. Both contribute to the prevention of diabetes mellitus and concurrently support loss of excess weight. Especially in overweight patients, experts have found a strong hormonal adjustment. Forgoing food leads to improved mood due to increased release of the happiness hormone serotonin, as well as endogenous opiates and morphine. Because of increased serotonin levels, we experience a heightened emotional vibration that critically supports our body's healing. I got to the power of fasting in 2013. A short period after I came back from Brazil and had a long therapy with a breast tumor medication, Anita told me to not only try switching diets but she introduced me together with my brother to the method of fasting. It had been two years since I tried to come back to full health but my body did not react that well. He mirrored how i reacted to mycellf and others. Tumours in male breast is rare but as it was running in my family we interpreted it to be a genetic risk. Living in the same patterns, living the same Karma as the ancestors.


I switched my diet from vegetarian to vegan. But there wasn't a big improvement and I physically felt exhausted. I had immense heat rushes, my humour was terrible and I suffered from my manic emotional waves. Probably my family and friends even suffered more. So I decided to fast and did it for a six-week period, some days only liquids, some days only water, fresh ginger tea, cabbage juice, and some days lots of fresh green and red juices. Some days soups and mashed veggies. I stopped consuming my compulsive thoughts and food choices... I felt my mind calming, I sensed the tumours in my breast decreasing and after the six weeks it was gone. After that experience I started to deepen my knowledge about this practice and it shows that we, from childhood on, have this deep wisdom within us to refrain from foods and listen to the body when it is needed.

Moderate fasting renews health in those who are sick or less than healthy. In addition, those who are healthy benefit from periodic fasting, by preventing sickness that has not yet arrived

—Hildegard von Bingen

If you feel drawn to fasting there are several ways of doing it. Find your individual choice and individual way of fasting. I invite you to inspire yourself from others, take valuable information and inform yourself, and most important, listen to your inner guidance.

N.B. Fasting is generally suitable for everyone and to start it is suggested to be carried out with the guidance of a naturopath, holistic physician or otherwise knowledgeable expert. One very important thing I want to mention here: trust your body. Science and experiences can serve as an inspiration for one's own path even though remember it is your individuality that has a personal way of expressing health, freedom and peace.

# 26. Fasting Method for Resetting Intuitive Consumption Behaviour

Today your body may need a breakfast, tomorrow a lunch and after tomorrow a dinner. Really you will consume intuitively in a timeframe; I noticed the earlier I ate I got earlier tired and the later I ate the more sleep I needed. The morning especially is to detox and utilise metabolic leftovers within the body. It's the time when I turn my body, the state of relaxation, into action. The parasympaticus which is as well the rest and digest mode to the sympaticus which is often referred as fight and flight. I recognise for myself that there are frames that I can use to improve general well-being and if we start to communicate with our cellular wisdom, with the language the body offers, then we may live life in a manner that's easier. To learn speaking with the body better and relearn the language I integrate fasting as soon that I sense that some communication is a little blurred.

Why do we not always understand what is good for our cells and our whole being? Because we consume from the moment we wake up till the night thoughts, sometimes we even eat and drink all day long. All that we consume the body will try its best to metabolise and as well try to utilise the leftovers in the intercellular space or false folded proteins and organelles which stay stuck and may just flow unproductively around. So the fast I utilise for myself consists only of teas and juices from healing, plant-derived sources. Is it possible to do a fast with soups as well? Yes, but consider that the less you give the body to digest the more energy it has to digest what is a leftover. If you feel like introducing yourself to any fasting method be aware that you may only use plant-derived products as animal products decrease the body's flow capability by, for example, an overload of cholesterol and purin. A 'purin leftover' is turned into uric acid and then builds crystals that are stuck in the joints and cause pain and inflammation. Too much animal-derived cholesterol may create cholesterol crystals, which make the arterial wall inflexible from within. Foods and drinks that are responsible for a high uric acid level are milk and milk products, any alcoholic beverages, every type of fish, meats, such as bacon, veal, venison, turkey, and organ meats like liver, heart and kidneys. The cholesterol-rich foods are eggs, cheese, butter, generally milk products, fish, meats, organ meats and processed foods and sweets that include animal protein.

To help the body release those leftovers, as mentioned, I integrate within a 24h period a time of not eating. Another factor may be calcification; I feel science is a great tool to understand how we can first start with it but know that each body works in its individuality and only when your body and your mind is empty you may understand what's beyond it. The body deserves some moments to rest and even the mind. When I start a fasting period I as well am aware that I fast from consuming information as well. Only seeing the self as a whole being will allow to metabolise the past within the psychology and physiology. When I live intuitively and metabolise the past I start to be able to see and sense what may be of service to myself totally effortlessly. It happens without an intellectual conversation, it's feeling the connection to 'mycellf'. I invite myself to myself without consumption. Fasting for me is to unlearn what we believe about food and start to communicate with a wisdom beyond intellect.

I always wondered why my body was drawn to some foods; in the past when I didn't listen to my cellular wisdom I would just eat what came on the plate or what I thought I should eat even when I sensed that it wouldn't be good for my general well-being. Now sometimes I will order in the restaurant and eat the whole plate as I feel like or only eat from the plate what I sense would nourish my cells. The same I do while fasting and I always find it inspiring to feel how what I consume interacts with my body and the research that science has revealed about it. It shows me that the communication with the body can be a practical tool to integrate what science is just discovering now. So how to begin a fast?

I start with an intestinal cleanse. I use 1ml castor oil per each kg that my body has and mix it with 2ml fresh squeezed pomegranate per each kg that my body weighs. Sometimes I as well use a sour berry juice like cranberry which I make freshly at home or I buy a 100% juice in the organic store. I personally love to go to nature or an organic store and communicate with it before I consume something and then research what has been revealed. The ancient Egyptians were one of the first who took notes about the medical benefits of castor oil. Besides the cleansing and relaxing effect of the digestive tract it was used for conditions all over the skin, even tumours, especially close to the breast surface. I feel how the liver as well benefits from a cleanse with castor oil. Pomegranate is a very strong antioxidant agent. All the richness in anthoyanins, flavonoids and vitality substances enrich our physiology with vibrant energy. The strong anti-inflammatory properties support the regulation of bad moods and stressful days. Besides that it is a great helper to make the stroma intercellular liquid more agile. We need that to be able to better metabolise and transport metabolic leftovers within our body. When I drink pomegranate I feel how my cells get new agility, vitality and start to get in the mood of regeneration. Important for me is to drink freshly squeezed if available or enrich it with some live cultures. Especially to support my body in keeping the regeneration mode on pomegranate is a great friend. It has shown that in prevention and treatment of several conditions, from many different types of cancer, to rheumatic conditions, cardiovascular conditions, osteoarthritis and many more, pomegranate gives the body new life. Yes, it is as well the fruit of rejuvenation as it improves the skin's healing abilities and supports the cells in reproduction. The beneficial effects that come from the various bioavailable constituents influence a beneficial gene expression. Cranberry with its richness in phytochemicals supports the heart center and helps to ease cardiovascular conditions and cancer. Cranberry does not only have a rejuvenating antioxidative effect because of its electron donating ability but as well very strong anti-inflammatory powers. Cranberry is so kind that it even stands like a good friend beside us to intensify cellular apoptosis. It has shown to be a coach to modulation of protein synthesis and gene expression involved especially in the proliferation cell. It prevents bacterial adhesion and sliming like the formation of biofilms that lead then to infections. Cranberry's efficacy depends on the bioavailability of its phytochemicals which are perfectly working in fresh-pressed juice or berries.

When I do this I take a whole afternoon for myself. I need to stay close to a toilet as my body will understand this as a signal to cleanse from the leftovers in the digestive tract. So I mix the juice and the castor oil. For me it would be 65ml of castor oil and 130 ml of pomegranate juice and then I drink it at once. Then I drink a full cup of warm water and wait 1.5 hours to start drinking water again. Importantly, after ingesting the castor oil I never consume food within the same day. We can even have years of collected excrement that didn't leave the body. With this technique we let it all out. The best time for me to use it is around 2:00 – 3:00 p.m. as I will have enough time to let it all out and then sleep and recover. I have my last meal 3hours before so that the food is digested before I drink my cleansing elixir. I wouldn't do it later as it may result in a long night being married to the toilet rather than with your bedsheet. Please note that I personally think it is essential to do this cleanse for my body before I do the first fasting.

The next morning I wake up and feed into what would nourish my body's process of metabolising and transforming leftovers. So I can start with my schedule.

For the first time I used the following schedule:

After waking up for the first three days I take a half teaspoon of bicarbonate in a mug and pour a little boiling water on top then a little cold water. The time of consumption of tea and water when I do a three-day fast is from 11-17:00 after and before I do not consume any water and tea to support my body with freshening up the cellular water. I will elaborate a little more on dry fasting later.

If I fast within a period of three days I may drink only water and herbal tea. Fasting longer I have a different routine which changes depending on my cellular needs. For an introduction I will use this fasting method.

20 min after my bicarbonate I drink a Detox Tee (never hot tea)

11:00 200ml cabbage juice (never pasteurised)

12:00 coconut water or herbal tea 100ml

13:00 herbal tea

14:00 coconut water or herbal tea 100ml

15:00 200ml cabbage juice

16:00 lemon water 100ml water and one lemon squeezed in after you wash your mouth with water

17:00 detox tea

18:00 cabbage juice

19:00 herbal tea

20:00 100ml cabbage juice

After only water.

I do a longer fast once or twice a year as I feel listening to the cellular needs more beneficial for me. Mostly I consume in a day within a time window of one to six hours. Longer fasts need a long time to reintroduce food again. I personally love to do it in summer as fresh fruits and vegetables are available in abundance and the body recognises what is naturally ripe and is better able to metabolise. Some people love to break the fast with a fresh cooked vegetable soup and eat that for two or three days, (never hot, always max 40 degrees when you eat it.) When I consume cooked foods to introduce meals again after fasting I eat it within two to three hours so that I still can absorb the life energy of the food. If you consume foods that were stored longer than three hours give the food your full attention and be sure that it will nourish you. Before I eat any food I give my gratitude to it and tell it to be nourishment for me.

'May all my cells be nourished and vitalised, thank you.'

Fasting is a spiritual practice to metabolise what has been practised. When I fast I take time for myself. To invite me and reset what it is that really nourished me. I invite myself to go from consumption to metabolism of what I have consumed. It is a practice to create a space to reflect deeper. It makes me unpractise what I practised. I invite myself fully.

# 27. Fasting, Mental Health and Exorcism

How is exorcism explained? 'Exorcism is the religious or spiritual practice of evicting demons or other spiritual entities from a person, or an area, they are believed to have possessed.'

'Mental health illnesses such as Huntington's Disease (HD), Tourette syndrome and schizophrenia were believed to be signs of possession by the Devil. This led to several mentally ill patients being subjected to exorcisms. This practice has been around for a long time, though decreasing steadily until it reached a low in the 18th century. It seldom occurred until the 20th century when the numbers rose due to the attention the media was giving to exorcisms. Different belief systems practice exorcisms in different ways.' Wikipedia Exorcism & Mental health

So how did that work? Not only by bondage and speaking an exorcism. It was a way of showing and teaching the possessed one with affirmations (Latin exorcism) that they are more than what they think and believe. The radical way of exorcism was as well including no food and often no water for several days. So it was the combination of no food and water and affirmations that healed the possessed ones. Fasting induces lowering the inflammation and intensifying self-healing abilities but as well the metabolisation of stored traumata that helps us perceive the world differently. Neuroplasticity plays a key role here. Healing the brain. That is very suggestive thus very fragmented. Considering that exorcism was not only healing but as well taking life away.

# 28. Dry Fasting When I Consume Nothing Else but Myself

There are two types of fasting: dry fasting and water fasting. In dry fasting one goes without taking food or water. The criteria for naming it dry fasting is because it does not allow the intake of any water. Dry fasting can be divided into soft dry fasting and hard dry fasting. In dry fasting, the individuals who are fasting do not allow their bodies to come into contact with water in any way. They avoid activities such as swimming, washing of dishes, taking showers or baths, and brushing their teeth. On the other hand, in soft fasting, the people fasting allow their bodies to come into contact with water. When one engages in a dry fast, the skin pores acquire a huge capability of absorbing water through the skin. Water fasting is a kind of fasting where the individual does not consume food but consumes water. I always love to include what beautiful research science is giving us, therefore I want to elaborate a little more on dry fasting.

In dry fasting, the body does not receive any external source of water. Therefore, it has to synthesise its own water essential for the survival of the cells. The serum is usually made up of saturated fats. Based on the chemical structure, a saturated compound is one with the maximum possible number of hydrogens attached to the carbons. In dry fasting, most of these hydrogens are released, so resulting in metabolising unsaturated fats. Like explained above the hydrogens are released into blood. On the other hand, human beings breathe in oxygen. When two hydrogens combine with an oxygen atom, they form a water molecule. Even if the body is able to form in a way 'homemade' water like in a short dry fast or cellular respiration at this point water is essential for life. Interestingly even when one is fasting, the person is able to urinate due to the water that is internally formed by the body. It is consumption and transformation of stored informations within me.

In addition, since the body is not receiving any food or water, the body will try to break down cells, especially those that are not very efficient, in order to acquire water and food needed for the metabolic activity in the body. This replacement of damaged cells with new cells with release of energy is referred to as autophagy. The rate of autophagy is very high in dry fasting as compared to water fasting. This is especially important with trauma that's stored in the stroma as it can be metabolised during a dry fast. Moreover, when one is dehydrated, there exists a certain vacuum in the body. This vacuum is due to the difference in pressure between the cell cytoplasm and the surrounding of the cell. This difference in pressure occurs as a result of the difference in volume between the intracellular fluid and the extracellular fluid. This results in the cell releasing its wastes and toxins into the extracellular space. The water that was formed internally by the body then washes these toxins resulting in their removal from the body, mostly through urination.

So what about dry fasting and inflammation?

One could see inflammation is like an immune reaction that occurs in the body in response to cellular injury. Fasting has been shown, through many studies, to cause a reduction in swelling. This happens through reduction and inhibition of a precursor of inflammation known as Leukotriene B4. This leukotriene is involved in a series of processes that result in inflammation. These processes include oxidative metabolism, the release of enzymes and stimulation of the migration of neutrophils to the site of injury so resulting in the aggregation of the white blood cells, so inflammation. Thus, through fasting, these series of events are inhibited, thus prevention of inflammation. However, it should be noted that fasting can only be used for a short period of time in controlling inflammation as prolonged fasting can lead to negative health effects since the body will be unable to meet its metabolic demands.

Every child when it gets sick it doesn't want to eat or even drink very often. So cultural beliefs make us overwrite this amazing wisdom of strengthening the self-healing activities. So it can always be beneficial to listen to the body's intuitive intelligence and combine it with what science reveals.

How do I dry fast? I take 16-24 hours where I don't consume any liquid or food which gives the body the chance to metabolise even old water and magically produces new fresh water for the body itself. Sometimes a little longer depending on how my body reacts. How does that work? If you look at the molecular structure of water it has hydrogens and oxygens.

Keep in mind that most of the fat in the body is saturated fat which has hydrogens. So what does that mean? To just quickly repeat it, what happens is that when the body is in a dehydrated state like what happens in a dry fast it breaks down the fat and releases the hydrogen. The hydrogen from the metabolised fat gets into the bloodstream and combines with oxygen that we breathe in which then creates $H_2O$, otherwise called water. It's the body that creates water itself in this process. So the old water within the body gets replaced with fresh, homemade water that the body itself has synthesised.

Not only normal fasting but as well even more dry fasting works as an 'anti-inflammatory practice. Did you ever see a dried fruit, bread or plant having fruit flies or fungus around it? That's it. There are none. Did you ever think why it is this way? Inflammation is dependent on the water flow. Inflammation loves water. So does that mean I should put myself into a fruit dryer or don't drink any more water? The thing is, if I try to temporarily reduce inflammation very quickly there is no easier way than just getting rid of water. There are concepts like dry fasting which promote that. Again, it doesn't mean that anyone should walk around all the time dehydrated. It's just a reminder that inflammation and all inflammatory responses require water to initiate that. Having a short fast without consuming water reduces inflammation within the body. It is a great practice to metabolise 'the flames of inflammation' and recycle the body's metabolic leftovers. What a wonderful mechanism.

# 29. Happiness

We all have heard it hundreds of times that people who are happier can achieve better lives with more outstanding outcomes, they are financially successful, live in generally supportive relationships. It even seems that happiness is related to mental health and even physical health which is correlated in our times with longevity. I sense that very often there is a social call to do everything to become happy, lots of practices and improvement. Is it a need to run behind happiness as something to achieve? Generally it seems that happiness itself is a ground base that predicts positive labelled outcomes, rather than simply resulting from the outcome itself. When I personally speak about happiness it is the happiness that comes from the joy of being, not the opportunity to identify one's self through accomplishing or gaining anything, as this may not last. It is a deep state that gets wired into the cells because when we live intuitively we cannot have an unhappy life or suffer.

In several parts in this book it is my invitation to you. See the opportunity to feel, see and experience how emotions manifest in health. If we live intuitively we can without any of that data access the wisdom that already knows all this. How can I be sure about something so vast? To find all those conclusions I have just felt into my body and looked at the moments that would more stand out in my imagination. Look at what I have learned from it and then research about it within me and in the external world. We don't need science if the intention of it is to identify with it to navigate our life. Science has actually a beautiful meaning which for me would be like to 'know'; therefore, it has two sides. The intuitive that knows and the intellectual that knows as well. We can use it as an intellectual tool to inspire each other to learn that we are more than the physical limitations and more than the limitations our mind gives us. Yes, again, living intuitively allows us to understand this wisdom our body is telling us and all this scientific knowledge can help us dive into it with the mind and use the mind as a creator of knowledge, new science and to perceive things from a new spot.

When our cells are not open and haven't metabolised the past, we still have old experiences stuck within us which then filter the capacity to distinguish what is from the past, the future and what reality is offering us. Those factors increase inflammation. The inflammation of my whole 'cellf'. For me, every moment I'm not in freedom and peace is when I'm pressing myself down. When I'm not expanding my cells, when I'm not expanding myself is for me depression. Sometimes I hear depression is a condition which has to have an immense impact. But for me, depression is always when I'm not uplifted and open for life. I think the word depression itself and its origins have that beautifully explained. So in Latin depression comes from deprimere 'press down'. Pressing down myself and others. Yes, that is what depression does. So why speak about my perspective of depression? Because for me that main cause of depression is if you remember inflammation, one could say cellf-inflammaton which then inhibits me to experience life, every new moment. I experience life within a highway that has no exit. Life becomes locked and I believe I can't change it. But yes we can, which the beautiful process of neurogenesis is showing us.

What is neurogenesis? Breaking down the word, it is the 'formation of something'—genesis. I love that description. Let that sink in, the formation of something. Just something, nothing specific, no highway without exit. The second part is neuro which then is relating to nerves. So instead of something is getting badly on my nerves, it is just the formation of something on my nerves. Can you sense the freedom of that? So remember I mentioned that when depression is me when I'm not in freedom and peace and when I'm pressing myself down. Depression and the false interpretation of reality happens when I'm not able to lift myself up and not do the formation of something but yes, do the formation of what makes me suffer and that happens without being aware of it. That happens when I believe my mind, the one that loves to show me imagination instead of reality.

How to arrive in reality? Let me ask you. How do you know where you are right now? Do you sense it? How does the body make us experience our surroundings? It depends on the capability of our nervous system. Nature has so much wisdom and once again I want to mention that this is an invitation to rather be the formation of something than the formation of a fixed belief. Those cages of beliefs may look beautiful in the beginning but as well can put us down to not be able to spread our experience in other directions. As I have mentioned the nervous system is the one with the capability to let us experience what is around us. But if there is something within us, a stored trauma, belief or conviction which misinterprets if there is danger we inflame and burn. If we rely on the intuitive wisdom of our cells and use this fire as a fuel we get to know how to act in that situation, use that fire and try our best to not burn and transform the fire of others so that they don't burn as well.

In a situation that a threat is recognised—we all know and have felt in a dangerous situation—the heart rate increases, we feel the blood flowing faster, we get a rush, and see and hear things clearer. The cells, especially muscles, help to compete with danger by receiving more nutrients and blood flow. Each part of the body has the beautiful individuality of a different kind of specialised cell which could be nerve cells and glial cells. The nerve cells, which are called neurons, generate the signals that are then quickly transmitted throughout long distances in the body. Then we can react quickly. The glial cells are as well important and necessary in the nervous system and mostly work by supporting the neurons. They are like best friends.

So coming again to the term neurogenesis. If you recall the formation of something in the neurons was often thought to be not possible in adults. We really thought that there is no way of generating new neurons in adults. That is what I have experienced in my new birth moment. I left the highway and started to ride down all the beautiful valleys. Looking at reality from so many different perspectives. I know that we all have the capability to create those new roads. I see it every day. Intuition shows me that it is possible. When I make myself and others small it is as well in the physiology that this manifests. Depression which is initiated by childhood trauma, for example, abuse, shrinks not only the perspective in a psychological sense but as well in the physiology.

I'm fascinated how scientists got the idea to measure the volumes of the hippocampus, a region in the brain which is linked to the limbic system and is associated with learning and emotions and as well involved in the formation of new memories. I wondered how they could do that so the idea was to look at the difference of participants with current unipolar major depressive disorder then participants with a history of prepubertal physical and/or sexual abuse and some without a history of prepubertal abuse and some healthy non-abused volunteers. So to measure the brain regions in depressed woman with and without abuse and healthy non-abused participants to compare.

The interesting part comes now. Recall the meaning of depression? Yes, 'press down'. Always when I press myself or others down I make myself smaller, and that is literally. So they measured the volume of the hippocampus, the region associated with learning, emotions and formation of new memories, just to recap. What they found out is that in the depressed participants with childhood abuse they had an 18% smaller mean left hippocampal volume compared to the ones that were in the non-abused depressed group and they had a 15% smaller mean left hippocampal size than the healthy participants.

You know that just blows my mind every time how dramatically the body loves to mirror what we psychologically experience. Something even more to consider here is that in these specific findings it seems that a smaller volume in the hippocampal area could also be a risk factor when it comes to developing a psychiatric disorder, specifically after exposure to overwhelming stress. And with overwhelming stress I would interpret as not metabolised stored trauma in our cells.

The purpose of a debate is not to win,
because there is nothing to win. There
is only reason to collaborate
perspectives so both parties can arrive
at a more dense inner standing

—Reiss Davies Ausar

As you probably already have felt here I love play with the perspective from pathogenesis which has this beautiful description as the manner of development of a disease. Which if we do not have cell-awareness of can become a manner, then to salutogenesis which I interpret as the manner of development of a health. The body is always interested in evolving and it won't ever stop as much as it can till it's time for us to transform and return. Here I invite you to look at all the data with an open heart. Increased neurogenesis to recover from early childhood trauma supports being able to live a life that's filled with reality, and reality for me is always kindness itself. For me and all that I have experienced living the intuition increases neurogenesis.

To become more practical and obtain some tools, is it possible to control neurogenesis, the formation of something new? Yes, it is. Let's look what does increase neurogenesis.

I would like to do a little exercise here. Just answer it to yourself. I will give you a couple of examples and you answer with increase and decrease. From what we have heard so far, any clue that the following six factors could increase neurogenesis?

**Learning**

**Sex**

**Stress**

**Sleep deprivation**

**Exercise**

**What you eat**

Yes, you guessed it: learning, sex, exercise and what we eat increases neurogenesis in the hippocampus. Here is a short list of what else has a beneficial effect to create new neurons: plant-based omega 3 fatty acids, calorie restriction, blueberries, folic acid, zinc, flavonoids, curcumin, intermittent fasting, terpenes. On the other side, what decreases neurogenesis? High sugar, high saturated fats, etanol (alcohol), even minimal amounts, a diet that's low in plant-derived vitamins such as A, E, B. Diet modulates emotional intelligence, mood and memory in the same direction as it modulates neurogenesis. So the effects of diet on emotional intelligence, mood, memory and general health are actually mediated by the production of new neurons in the hippocampus.

Let me invite you here to meditate with a little journaling; practice on it and reflect on your neurogenesis. Please use at least two minutes writing an answer for each question.

What is pressing me down?

What is lifting me up?

When is it that I have the manner of development of a condition?

When is it that I have the manner of development of a health?

I'm in love with science and I feel how beneficial it is to use the intellect, mind and thoughts in a constructive way. Even with all this wonderful information science provides listen to your non-judgemental intuition that will always bring, peace, freedom of mind and each physically possible expression of health. Real science is wisdom that's rooted deep within; we can use guidelines but on the road what really keeps us connected is our intuition.

Can you recall an experience, a painful situation or moment of suffering, even a moment that emotions just took over? A moment which you would say impacted you a lot. It could be a trauma in your childhood, something that just happened that gave you physiological pain or any other pain or suffering. It could be a discussion, a burn, a cut or any other moment that you remember, and since when you have learned to behave differently in a similar situation? Why am I asking you that? Because those moments interact with our behaviour. What does that mean? When having a traumatic moment or one that's not metabolised throughout our whole being this moment sticks to our neurons. When it's not metabolised it sticks with us like glue. And we behave, act and feel according to a specific moment in the past in a moment after that. That can happen moments, years, or centuries after that.

There are some neurons called interneurons which are actually the most numerous classes in processing information from simple to complex triggers in the brain. I look at those neurons as the ones that help us with conclusions but if they are glued on past experiences our conclusions are just faded past-experience interpretations instead of experiencing the beauty of reality. It's essential to learn and to take past information as references. We do that constantly but when the information is not metabolised and transformed as a source of wisdom then that is when the trauma is stuck in us. This can be from similar unpleasant experiences to extreme overwhelming moments that reoccur over and over again in life. It's like a karmic glue that lets us experience again and again what has happened and what didn't happen yet.

You may ask yourself what all this science and trauma has to do with intuition.

You remember that thoughts, beliefs and convictions filter our ability to listen to intuition? So here it comes. Beliefs are not something that we only have in our minds; actually all our cells in the body contain them. A trauma is a cellular belief that a specific moment, a specific sensory experience will cause harm. That includes sensory experiences created through imagination as well. Most beliefs are hardwired to protect us from harm. It's the natural intuitive response;

if, for example, a lion would jump by we would get triggered, produce lots of adrenaline, the digestion would stop, our pupils would dilate as well as heart and respiratory rate would increase without actively having to think about it. This is the physical intuition that provides us the information to do the best in moments that would be harmful for the physical body.

Yes, you've probably already guessed it; the same happens with traumata, emotional experiences and exciting events. The thing is, we often miss interacting intuitively because of the ways that we humans are presented in TV shows, movies, books, romantic stories, that we actually believe we should act in a similar manner, losing our individuality and acting instead of living life fully. Those beliefs of how we should act make us identify with any occasion and get value from the identification that this specific moment did to us. The egoic identity loves it to identify with beliefs, and those beliefs cause physiological responses that make us suffer the same or even can make us suffer more than the actual experience. So from this point I would love to invite you, if you feel connected to what was just explained, to meditate about it, reflect on it. Allow yourself to live intuitively. Do I believe that every trauma can be metabolised and turned into a source of wisdom? Yes, I do. Even if it is a belief. You want to know why? Because I have experienced the grace of receiving the guide to do it.

The method to release that stored information and process it is the 10-point exercise; if you have one trauma that you don't believe can be resolved, I tell you it can with recurring training of the 10 Point Intuition Cell-Awareness Method.

Intuition always provides us with simple solutions that have already been practised by other intuitive beings, mystics, healers, yogis and heath apostles. So to wrap it up besides the 10. Point methods that in my personal experience changes the way we perceive reality we utilize lifestyle changes that increase general health as an easy guideline to uncover and unfilter what we perceive. It helps us experience reality in all the beauty that it is provided to us.

The egoic identity is to the soul what the brain is to the heart.

# 30. Intuition and Illness

I always consider living intuitively as a way to have fun and enjoy all possibilities that life has to offer—good ones and bad ones. So let's look at those considered bad and good: how do those beliefs impact our physical and mental health?

If we don't live from the intuition we don't always recognise that we are often imprisoned in our beliefs. Those beliefs can create nocebos and placebos. Intuition is to recognise what the individual placebo is. So let's take a quick break to understand what science means with placebo and nocebo. What does that mean? That our convictions, beliefs and thought patterns create the way we perceive ourselves and shape physical and emotional conditions. Intuition will allow you to become aware of your thoughts and words, and the thoughts and words of others.

Let this sink in:

In the beginning was the word.

A spell is spelled through spelling.

As you wish it shall be.

Find where you identify yourself with illness of any kind. Look at it, perceive it, connect to your intuition so you will gain freedom of mind to perceive reality. Our mind is so powerful it is the creator of our experience.


Cells always listen because in the beginning was the word. So switch the perspective on all what is missing. I just let objects, nutrition and people be seen as they are. I look at them with my two eyes and perceive reality. Intuition allows me to trust, to love and to be free. So if I believe that food is full of toxic substances and don't look at the facts with an open heart and mind I might unconsciously create a world of toxicity that's more beyond facts than what reality is. The same happens if I believe that a person is bad and wants to do me harm while that person is not in front of me. But here it comes again: what we believe in shapes the way we live. So here I invite you again to reflect on it, let what you just read sink in, take a deep breath and look at it with a non-judgemental mind. The 10 Point Intuition Cell-Awareness Method can be from all of the practices, a supporting tool to use intellect, to look behind beliefs and convictions, and look deeper within yourself. If you feel you can access your intuition just by going into yourself it is a great opportunity as well to do so now. Whatever you might feel, think or experience, even the slightest things in life, there is no reason to not love the kindness that reality provides to us.

The body is the temple of god. Who resides in it? Me.

Let's go a step further and find the Trojan horses that the egoic identity loves to create to fight with reality.

Being sure about the positive impact of something and meanwhile judging others for their way of not believing in what you are doing is a great puzzle piece to apply to the whole picture and see what intuition really is. This we could call a Trojan horse in our beliefs. Judging others and making them feel that they are living wrong is not intuition, it's the egoic identity that fights with what is and loves to create hierarchy to feel better than the other. But the egoic identity as well loves to make oneself feel worse than the other; how is that? Let's go to an example where illness plays a role. Let's say your friend starts to tell you how bad he is feeling with his life. To mirror his feelings you tell him an even worse story to amplify and create a hierarchy in which each tries to fight with the other subconsciously to make the other believe their personal story is much worse, or at least similarly bad to what the friend has told. Intuition allows you to listen mindfully and inspire your friend to connect to their intuitive source of wisdom. In other words, create an empathic, compassionate response.

If you think and feel that you have to care a lot about planet Earth, nature and animals and are trying your best to save the planet and start to judge others because they are not that compassionate and caring, that isn't your intuition speaking, that's a Trojan horse.

If you care about your health, body and mind through workouts, good food and healthy living and judge others because they are not caring that much or are not that compassionate about health and body culture in general, that isn't your intuition speaking, that's a Trojan horse.

If you feel you shouldn't consume anything that doesn't support your general well-being, such as negative news, unhealthy foods, unethical behaviour but judge others because they are unethical, unhealthy and unaware, that isn't your intuition speaking, that's a Trojan horse.

If you feel that there is a type of music that benefits your physical state and enjoy to feel the good energy that it brings to you and judge others because they are not listening to maybe calm, relaxing or dance and happiness music, that isn't your intuition speaking, that's a Trojan horse.

If you feel how immensely it increases the state of peace while we live from our intuition and not the egoic identity and judge those who don't follow the non-judgemental path, that isn't your intuition speaking, that's a Trojan horse.

So a Trojan horse is a program that's created by the egoic identity because the egoic identity loves to fight with all that is. It's so dramatic and does very well indeed. If you nourish yourself with the wisdom of your intuition, for example, through unpractising beliefs with the practices provided in this book or any other practice that helps you unpractise beliefs, you will be a creator of peace. We all long for connection and the only way to connect is through intuition which guides us the way to what's beyond connection and disconnection.

## The Belief in the Power of Illness

To live intuitively I don't need to believe in illness, the same way that I don't need to believe my imagination of **how health should look**. Notice and get aware of defence mechanisms that create a judgemental pattern against illness. It is a guide to perceive if it comes from the egoic identity or the intuition. It's to notice the manner of creating conditions. Remember, intuition is never judgemental. It gives me the opportunity to look at it, yes. And, yes, to treat it the best way possible. It as well leads me to get support and help if needed. From a three-dimensional view we can be in a degenerative state if we believe something and then our cells believe it. But the physical expression itself even on the way of degeneration is always drawn to evolve the best way that this very moment can give it. Salutogenesis is being 'holy'. Being in health and if you recall, it is the manner of creating health. Let's see what the word holy means literally. From hailagaz its translation would be holy and bringing health. From Proto-Germanic hailagaz it means healthy and whole. Living intuitively is being holy, bringing health to you and health to everyone else. Being one with all that is. Seeing all selves, all bodies, all minds and the souls not as separate. Seeing that we are all interconnected. Always. In all ways. How did I get to the word holy besides from living holistic? After my rebirth experience the first church I have visited, I saw this beautiful paintings and statues with the shining ring around the head. One painting had a stream coming down from heaven with a white pigeon above the head. Which is considered the messenger of the holy spirit. That is what I felt since that moment, i saw my life from above now. I got gifted with self-awareness, the opportunity to feel that always existing presence within me that is looking to myself from within and from without myself. I could sense since that moment what it meant to have reality lightened up and when I saw this drawing I understood what holy meant for the first time. Understanding, learning and integrating the holiness, the completeness of oneself.

# 31. Flow Like Water

Water is the transport vehicle in our body to help nourish every cell in this wonderful organism. As I gained the gift of living from my intuition I felt quickly how my body would react differently to drink choices and food choices than it had before. My sensitivity to nourish this body with what it really asks for is mastered when I live from intuition. I sensed that all I consume interacted with the patterns that I had accumulated in all the years living in this body.

Intensely I felt it when drinking. Once my brother brought water from a fountain for me; as I saw it I just felt the urge to drink it without even knowing it was from a fountain. Then when he gave me tap water and I drank it, it blew my mind. It felt like my body didn't want to drink it anymore. This expanded to water in bottles as I started to sense there is something in the fountain water that really nourishes me intensely, letting me see clearer what intuition was telling me. As funny as it sounds, if we accept the natural flow that fountains provide us, the body embraces its health. So as I started to travel more and always felt this wonderful call from fountains while living in the city and could not always access fresh water, I decided to research more about it. I found information that I would interpret why I felt that my intuition was speaking louder when consuming water from a fountain. I came to realise the substances that couldn't be filtered out of the water, so with the passion I have about biology, my friend, Anita-Juliane Winkler Green, a bioinformatics scientist, and I started to do more research on water that was tested in laboratories.

It seems the water cleaning techniques we have are still improving so we tried to find out why and how they could be improved. We both love science and the beauty of what humans can create. So we started to filter what on a physical level as opposed to the mental level would be the other puzzle piece of living more intuitively. Here you can find a list of what we found in water from medications that interact with our hormonal state and mental behaviour and can be seen as endocrine disruptors in this setting.

Bezafibrat 1) lipid-lowering agent

Carbamazepine 2) anti-epileptic drug

Clofibric acid 3) lipid-lowering drugs

Dichlofenac 4) analgesics

Ibuprofen 5) analgesics, antipyretic, anti-inflammatory

Metoprolol 6) beta-blockers

Phenazone 7) anti-inflammatory

Propyphenazone 8) analgesics

Sotalol 9) beta-blockers

Sulfamethoxazole 10) antibiotic

And many more...

To really understand the impact of the mixtures of all these medications together in one glass is very difficult with the now existing science. Medications are a wonderful biomedical tool to treat conditions. If we do not have any conditions physicians will not prescribe medications because of the side effects in the physical body. Sounds logical, doesn't it? So what **I want to mention** concerning drinking water is to be aware of the physiological responses that endocrine disruptors have, as we know now that endocrine disrupting chemicals can interfere with the hormonal system. It's not totally clear yet what happens when consuming those many medications and substances dissolved in water. But it seems to be that those disruptors produce in the body adverse developmental, neurological, reproductive, as well as cardiovascular, metabolic and immune effects in humans, which can range from substances that are considered natural to man-made. They seem to be thought to cause the endocrine disruption. This as well is including dioxin, several pharmaceuticals, dioxin-similar compounds, pesticides, and components of plastics such as bisphenol A (BPA) and phthalates, and many more.

What else I found very interesting is that this interference from endocrine disrupting chemicals can block or mimic the actions of hormones and then be causing a wide range of effects that could be pulling down the cellular health.

Those side effects can be compared in the same way as thoughts interact in our physiology. Even if our body can adapt to many different external and internal factors, having this wonderful science is a good intellectual guidance to become more aware of how consumption from unnatural sources interacts with the biological system of our body.

Every cell which builds with the DNA the organs has the same essence than a cell from a tree, a plant, another human or another organism. We all stem from the same source. The cells within our body that swim within the cell water or intercellular space are the road of the lymphatic system to our smallest capillaries. Hormones, leukocytes, nutrients and many more move through this road. If the road is blocked by plugs, flow is limited. The cellular metabolism gets stock and the destination of hormones, nutrients and cellular helpers may not be reached. The main reasons for those blockages are parasites, bacteria, fungal infection, viruses, not enough cellular water and movement, sugar, animal derived proteins, medication leftovers in tap water, no fasting periods, negative thoughts and stress.

Stress even alters the alkalinity of the body, important to keep in mind when the body gets inflamed. All those factors can lead to disharmony in the digestive tract where the parasites and unmetabolised protein molecules can enter the bloodstream. The blood gets thicker and plugs start to hold on the capillary walls. Even metabolic leftovers aren't now digested anymore by our cellular helpers, they just keep swimming within the intercellular space. To keep the capillary system clear I personally love to do a fast. Not only physiological blockages are stuck here but as well beliefs and traumas that we don't metabolise love to make our body their home.

Drink where a horse stills its thirst, a horse will never drink bad water. Go to bed where a cat sleeps, eat the fruit that a worm touched, grab fearless mushrooms, where gnats and mosquitoes sit down. Plant a tree where a mole burrows, build a house in the square where the snake warms, dig a well where the birds nest on hot days, go to bed and get up with the chickens, and so on. You get a golden grain for the whole day, eat more green so you will have strong legs and a persevering heart like an animal. Go swimming often, then you will feel like a fish in the water on the earth.

Often look to the sky and not under the feet so your thoughts will be clear and easy. Silence instead of talking, so the silence will inhabit your soul, your mind will be peaceful and calm.

# Center Of Intuition

There is actually a center or channel of intuition in the body. Yes, it is the pineal gland. The pineal gland is the connection link between our external environment and the movement of internal body systems. This tiny but important and powerful gland is in connection with the world around us. So this amazing pineal gland takes information from our environment and translates or converts it into signals that are chemical or electrical. The pineal gland is considered the master gland of the hormonal system (endocrine system). It resides in the middle of the brain and between the two eyes. Its capacity to convert light, temperature and magnetic environmental factors just mirrors for me why it is called the third eye.

The pineal gland is often called the center of the sixth sense, which is the intuition. In integrative medicine the pineal gland is seen like the gatekeeper that masters the transcendence of the five senses.

This little gland is calcified by a halogen called fluorine. I had been wondering why I would feel different drinking different bottled waters and drinking different tap waters so I started to research more about it. One funny thing I found is that fluorine has the highest electronegativity of all elements. When I read that I was just laughing because when I started to personally test between distilled water with and without fluorine I could sense that the lightness and clarity within my body would get negatively heavier after consuming the water that had salt with fluorine added. My favourite is spring water as it is high in life energy, it nourishes all our cells. When I'm traveling and distilling water I always add a little bicarbonate, sometimes even a little salt or fruits, which I leave overnight. So interesting is that when it comes to fluoride it seems to be very widely distributed everywhere in nature like in the air, soils, rocks and water. The manmade version which is a fluorine compound is super often in the manufacture of ceramics as well. Besides that in pesticides, refrigerants, aerosol propellants, as well in glassware, and the famous Teflon cookware. It seems to be generally an unwanted byproduct of aluminum. What I found very interesting, it seems that some researchers conclude fluoride has seemingly a potential to cause adverse human health issues.

# 32. Spring Water

Water of natural springs which serve as drinking water have a non-pathogenic microflora with regenerative properties. The potential presence of non-pathogenic bacterial species supports the body's immune system and symbiosis with beneficial bacteria. Compared to bottled water, refined spring water is likely to produce molecular mediators that even play a role with the wound-healing process. You probably have heard about springs with healing abilities besides the non-pathogenic bacterial species: it is the DNA-rich so-called 'dark matter' that contributes to the healing abilities. It's a spaceless not coded DNA sequence that has 'free energy to create'. You can imagine it like a modelling clay which you normally need someone to shape but this clay is taking its shape when it finds its creator; without having to be shaped, it shapes itself without any effort. All on this 3-D world is codependent on another mechanism. The benefits of spring waters have been demonstrated for thousands of years. It was used for the treatment of actual pathologies, strengthening the physiological self-healing abilities to gain back general health.

The molecular mechanisms of spring water indicates the body to respond with its anti-inflammatory and regenerative abilities. Or one could say that those abilities come from the spring water. The trend of the highly sanitised society and disinfection explains the huge increase of immune disorders.

In the last decades microorganisms and bacteria that went into symbiosis were recognised as dangerous for the human body. Not only the wisdom of ancient times but as well current scientific interest increased in understanding the position of microbiota for an increased vision of medicine. Nature knows it best: drinking spring water is high in vitality. It has pure healing abilities and strengthens and detoxes the human body. Spring waters are high in microorganisms that produce vitamins and help the body synthesise those. Remember that science can be the bounce-back whenever there should be a moment of cluelessness. Allow yourself to utilise science as a tool to strengthen your natural intuitive ability. It is about bridging intuitive wisdom practices and modern biomedical research. Living intuitively supports in life to bring out a holistic life.

# 33.  Intuition and the River

To elaborate here I would just like to tell you how nature is my biggest inspiration. So often there can be moments that challenge us and even trying our best to integrate and live what we feel sometimes it's hard to say yes to what we want and no to what we don't want and to understand the difference when it is that I want or don't want and when it is just a belief that I want or don't want.

Take a moment, arrive. Invite yourself to yourself. Imagine a river, clear, beautiful water, flowing in the valley, the water always finds its way. Now some kilometres further there are big stones in the way of the water, the water gets wilder and the water finds its way. Some kilometres further there is a waterfall, the water gets louder and stronger, the water finds its way. Some kilometres further the sun is getting stronger and stronger, water starts to evaporate, the river gets less and water finds its new way. Some kilometres further there is rain starting, very strong and the river gets full again, the water finds its way. Some kilometres further the land is very dry and the water just gives itself to the dry earth, effortless, the water finds its way. The river is empty now. Some kilometres further clouds are passing by and snow starts to fall, the water finds its own way.

Water has in every situation its own expression, never the same, always similar and constantly flowing. When the path gets rude water adapts, when the path gets calm water adapts, when the path gets dry water gives and if it's too dry to give it transforms its structure and gives for whoever is receivable. It's never destructed, it's always transformed.

Knowing others is intelligence;
knowing yourself is True wisdom.
Mastering others is strength;
mastering yourself is True power

—Lao Tzu, Tao Te Ching

So often when we go into topics that concern our individual health we can fall out of intuition and listen just to the egoic, judgemental and negative mind. Keep in mind while reading that living from your intuition will lead you to understand, see and experience reality in a non-judgemental way. We can use science as an intellectual program to embrace this beautiful body that was given to us as a gift to express ourselves in the material world. What I often do in this book is try to interpret intellectually what wisdom my body is giving me. Your intuition will show you that there is actually nothing that really can harm you and at the same time it shows you a caring, loving and gentle way to live a life that's beneficial for physiological and mental health.


Nature provides us with all gifts to clarify not only our beliefs but what's stored in the body. To clear the body from stored old knowledge, minerals, substances and traumas like mentioned above, one option to transform the information is fasting. The body metabolises what's not needed and releases or transforms most of it. There is a fruit called sour plump or tamarind which seems to support the body to eliminate excess and unneeded fluoride from the system. With this wonderful intellectual knowledge we can help the body to 'activate' the sixth sense, our intuition. This is an opportunity to reflect on all what we digest, not only mentally but physiologically like food, drinks and cosmetics.

While I do not have access to a fresh water fountains always when I travel I personally drink mostly freshly distilled water or my body draws me to water that nourishes my cells directly, mostly from high-water-content fruits and veggies that nourish me with the perfect equilibrium of minerals to 'flow like water' mentally and physically. Only your body can know what is good for you. So practising awareness of what we are consuming can be a possible gateway for a physiologically and mentally healthy experience. Notice that there is no practice needed to arrive in the present moment, nor to experience your intuition. Intuition is always everywhere. In my point of view we all have this gift to experience it in any given moment.

The thing we tell of can never be found by
seeking, yet only seekers find it

—Sufi wisdom

Where else does the word impact our external world? Let's look at an investigation taken by Masaru Emoto and his perspectives. He was a Japanese author and researcher who was convinced that human consciousness is having an effect on the molecular expression of water. Emoto's work around so-called pseudoscience hypotheses included the belief that water is reacting to positive and negative emotions and that a prayer or words could clear polluted water by positive visualisation. Masaru Emoto was a Japanese author, researcher and entrepreneur who said that human consciousness has an effect on the molecular structure of water. Emoto's conjecture evolved over the years, and his early work revolved around pseudoscientific hypotheses that water could react to positive thoughts and words and that polluted water could be cleaned through prayer and positive visualisation. His claim was that photographs of ice crystals from water that has been treated with different words and intentions would show a difference in the general structure.

Emoto was convinced that water was a 'blueprint for our reality' emotions which he considered as 'energies' and as well 'vibrations' could then change the physiological expression or structure of water. Emoto actually made the claim that water exposed to what he thought was positive speech and thoughts would result in a variety of visually 'pleasing' crystals which would be formed as soon as the water had been frozen and that on the opposite negative thoughts, words or intentions would create 'ugly' formations as soon as becoming frozen.

So is there any study taken that supports this as it is mostly considered pseudoscientific? For me, as soon as I speak from an intention that is not curiosity or peace I feel that the water within my cells, everywhere in my body starts to change. It feels like it is getting thicker and flow itself is not there anymore. When I close myself with negative thoughts I'm not receptive to the beauty of life anymore. Something that I recognised is that when I'm grateful for the water that I drink, when I infuse it with positive intention, when I use the power of my placebo, yes, then water holds deep power within.

When I started to look deeper in the topic of intention and water I found in a research that water 'treated' with intention can affect ice crystals. There was the control water which was not intentionally treated and the one that had been treated with intention. In the results it's indicated that those frozen crystals which came from intentionally treated water were given higher scores in a questionnaire for aesthetic appeal than those from the control water so this seems to be lending support to the hypothesis.

# 34. Clairvoyance and Intuition

Often clairvoyance is directly correlated with seeing future oracles, seeing and feeling auras, being able to perceive chakras, meridians and other entities and energies that reside around us. I sense clairvoyance is an opportunity to realise reality. Connect to the now and decide from there on. Intuition makes us in a sense all clairvoyant as we start to see things we did not realise before. We can see when the voices start to speak and know that we can identify with the positive or negative, thus knowing there is something beyond. It reveals the hidden. Makes the unseen seen. It clears all beliefs, filters and transforms blockages into wisdom sources. It is the gift of being able to recognise one's and others' feelings and actions as a mirror to each other. Super interesting is that if a person admits to knowing information that transcends from the sixth sense and the information creates fear, anger or stress in the one that is seeing, sensing or feeling it is for me reality that is filtered. Or I love to see it as well as a little romanticism or drama for the daily life. Thus reality that I see with my two eyes is always kind for me. So is there no such thing as fate? For me it just depends on one's romantic beliefs.

We all grow up with convictions and beliefs that cage us in a world that's identified with only the physical structure. Intuition makes us connect to our gift of clairvoyance, clairaudience, clairsentience, clairscent, clairtangency, and clairgustance or telepathic responses. That's my romantic response to what can't be seen from the other's eye. For me it is going in communication with all moments that have been, are now and might come. It's an open-hearted integration from a wisdom that's beyond intellectual belief. All those are gifts that come with intuition. We utilise intuition as a guide to integrate love, empathy and with it, the coming compassion. It's valuable to recognise that any expectation to be all knowing, all seeing and feeling doesn't come from intuition. Intuition leads us to an authentic life. It is easy to sense if visions or perceived information comes from the deep wisdom that intuition provides us or if it comes from the egoic mind that loves to create hierarchy. If what I sense, see or feel is not bringing freedom and peace with it, or is not spoken with the intention of curiosity and peace, that's the egoic identification of the mind.

Real clairvoyance washes away what creates this hierarchy. Real clairvoyance is seeing equality and individuality in everything. By living intuitively we naturally receive all information needed for us and others to evolve in the way it's supposed to. So recognise that stress, beliefs and convictions that arise out of the need to perform may lead to conceptual judgemental information that is not intuition. I mean, if you like a little drama from time to time to make the soup spicier, do and enjoy, thus know when the harmony is getting lost. Intuition can be accessed through stillness and alignment that is carried in every present moment though all the practical applications that you find in this book. Clairvoyance that's naturally gifted to all of us from intuition is the gate to free our human race and the world from all suffering. Living from within doesn't make you immune to human experience. It gently shows you the beauty of existence and teaches you to respond with curiosity and be conscious and self-aware. Intuition guides you to peace.

Once you recognise that you are able to experience all that others are experiencing it's always a good guide to keep in mind that any negative or judgemental expression of knowledge leads to suffering. There is a thin line between what is caring and loving information for a person to acknowledge and what information comes from a harmful perspective out of the egoic, judgemental mind. Intuition sends us often knowledge that is just for our personal 'notebook'. Here you can distinguish when it is a conviction that you feel that you have to give to a person as information or to answer a question, which mostly leads to a dogmatic outcome, or if this is knowledge of 'real intuition', that is always loving, in peace and freeing. To actually arrive in the present moment and see reality and how beautiful and kind it is. All information that we receive is a mirror that reflects the beauty of the now. There is no such thing as negative news if we live and speak from intuition. Always when we receive negative information that is judging what is we get the opportunity to look intellectually deeper into it.

# 35. Testing If the Information Comes From Intuition

What information did you receive?

How do you feel and react afterwards with this information?

Knowing your intuition is your best friend and always wants you and everyone to be in peace, does this match with the information?

So knowing that all that we experience is a mirror how could you turn it around, what would be the mirror for you?

Any other ways that you could turn it around?

It's valuable information to keep in mind that often when we work with strangers it might be easier to stay totally connected to our intuition. The real work starts when it gets to family, lovers or very old friends. They are our best teachers when giving information because of the convictions and because we think we have to compromise, or when we're speaking and giving out information the way that intuition always expresses it. To create freedom of mind, peace and health.

*Be still, and know...*

— *Bible*

Through intuition you will get to know the unfamiliar, the unknown where we can find new possibilities and opportunities to experience life that's always caring for us.

Real clairvoyance shows that all differences that are between us and all that try to divide us will never be stronger than love that unites everything. It makes us arrive in the present moment and inspire everyone around to live from their inner source of wisdom.

Often we are distrusting of our feelings and here I would love you to not distrust your negative or positive feelings. Use them as a guide to recognise what comes from your intuition. Often we are told that emotions are not that important as facts and reasons. We often try to control them, ignore, deny and hide them. I know that feelings matter in this particular time to be reminded where reality is happening. Intuition brings me to joy of life and I trust my intuition more than I trust in anything that my mind tries to make me believe. The reason I'm sharing this with you is to invite you to trust in your intuition. It is an opportunity to invite your convictions to open their perspectives to see there is no such thing as harm in this apparent world, ever. No.

Truth is something so noble that if God could turn aside from it, I could keep the truth and let God go.

—Eckhart von Hochheim

# 36. Parasites

Our body is inhabited by trillions of micro-organisms of several thousand different species. It is called the microbiome. Can you recall speaking about how our gut is influenced by processed foods? This is what I meant by microbiome. If the body is in a healthy, optimal state, they live together in perfect symbiosis. Everything stays in harmony and the balance is maintained as long as man lives according to the laws of nature, behaves and nourishes consciously and in an appropriate manner, because bacteria live through us and we through them. If we are overloaded with habitants that are closing our cellular health then we get the chance to review if we are living according to our individual intuitive health.

But if we start to go against our intuitive way of life, disregard the laws of nature, and change our habits of living intuitively to no longer meet our natural needs, that harmony quickly gets out of balance. Causes include antibiotics, environmental toxins (mercury, formaldehyde, fluoride), endocrine disruptors, a disturbed acid-base balance by a low-nutrient and acid-excess diet, overindulgence of sugar, nicotine, alcohol, drugs, persistent stress, lack of exercise, drug abuse, etc. The result can be a disturbed balance between pathogenic and beneficial bacteria that aid our digestion and metabolism. In the body an ideal sour and sick environment is formed, where the bacteria find everything that they need to grow and for rapid multiplication. The over-acidified and weakened body thus forms an ideal food base for fungi and parasites, whose task is to ensure that the out-of-balance body is decomposed. A fungal or parasitic infestation is therefore always the result of an unconscious lifestyle as well as wrong and unnatural dogmatic diet and beliefs of how we should care for our body instead of living individually intuitive.

# 37. Fungal Infection

The pathogenic fungi include yeasts (candida), moulds and dermatophytes. Mycotoxins, the excretions of fungi that can disturb the natural balance of physical health, especially affect the liver and kidneys. Fungi prefer to multiply in the small intestine because they do not need oxygen to survive. For example, yeast infection in the gastrointestinal tract causes bloating, diarrhea or constipation. Through the delicate intestinal mucous membranes, the fungi enter the bloodstream and reach every weakened organ.

What does all this knowledge have to do with intuition? You remember the part explaining about the microbiome and how it interacts with our emotional state, negative thoughts and inflammation? Yes, you got it. A not intuitive way of living can lead us to choices that aren't beneficial for our physical existence and take away the possibility to live from a conceptual physical health. This imbalance can lead to heart problems or chronic conditions. So when we are stressed, consume information that isn't coming out of the heart, aren't caring for this wonderful body, those parasites go in symbiosis with the body. When entering the bloodstream, this is called a systematic fungal condition where the whole body is affected. This means that already there are fungi, and other parasites are not far. Please read this topic with awareness and neutrality as to not induce an nocebo effect. Inviting images that are traumatic tend to close the cells so read this with curiosity as much as you are able as there can be several reasons the body goes in symbiosis. Our physiology always has the interest in evolving as best as he can in the given moment.

The parasites spread unhindered in our body and their metabolites not only pollute the intestine and the liver, but weaken our immune system and interfere in the way we feel, react and think. How can you recognise physically if you're not living the intuitive wisdom of your body? Whenever you or your body is not in natural balance. So how to recognise if there are visitors? They can lead to symptoms such as severe flatulence, chronic constipation, chronic diarrhea, neurodermatitis, obsessive negative thoughts, stomach and intestinal ulcers, etc.

As the parasites enter the bloodstream or lymphatic system, they actually interfere with all organs. The resulting inflammatory processes trigger serious illnesses in the respective organs. Can you remember the correlation between depression 'press down' and inflammation when the 'cellf' get inflammed?

And this kind of parasite overload leads to a chronic inflammatory process; there is a risk of a self-destructive overreaction of the mind and the immune system due to a complete overload. Such a development finally causes the emergence of so-called autoimmune conditions in which the immune system also attacks and destroys healthy tissue (such as Crohn's disease, arthritis, psoriasis, multiple sclerosis, etc.). Just a side note, cancers are also often the cause of chronic inflammation. Cancer is often described as well as a mostly genetic conditions or due to environmental factors but actually it is besides those two factors more a kind of metabolic condition regarding to the Warburg effect.

There are those who seek knowledge for the sake of knowledge; that is curiosity. There are those who seek knowledge to be known by others; that is vanity. There are those who seek knowledge in order to serve; that is Love

—Bernard of Clairvaux

The body goes in symbiosis with parasites to be able to metabolise through parasites' cell toxins and manage stress reactions that are taking over in the physical body. They take over as well because we aren't living intuitively. In the long run the physical expression of the body can stay in constant inflammation which leads to negative mindset and blocks us from seeing the beauty of life. If you remember inflammation leads to depression. So if, for example, depression is an inflammatory condition where does the inflammation come from? What I personally notice is that my organs respond to external factors a lot and as well to what I ingest. After my first fast I sensed that my body reacted differently to foods. So I started to feel more into my nutrition and did some research on about what other factors would increase that I physiologically would sense that I have more hormones that would feel positive or negative depending on my ingestion. So any feeling that was sensed to be pulling down I started to understand that it works like an inflammation in my body. What I found is that the pulling down or depression had to be associated with an inflammation in the whole body. I got very interested in that topic and it is still very inspiring for me to see the correlation from body to mind. Besides ingestion I found that there are as well factors that increase that inflammation, like psychosocial stressors, a not very biophoton-rich and mostly processed food diet, dental cares, sleep and vitamin D deficiency, no sports or generally no physical activity seems to increase as well the more negative associated feelings and emotions. Other factors which I could not relate to but seem to make an impact on increased inflammation and the down pulling are obesity, smoking, altered gut permeability, atopy. So, yes, besides food, low care for the own physiology it is also from stress that the body starts to experience inflammation which leads as well to any depressive disorder.

Negative emotions can filter our ability to experience miracles that are a great pointer and guide towards healing. Those negative emotions and thoughts block our energy and make us react in dogmatic behaviour. We start to fight with reality and live in imagination. If we are not led by intuition we always want to control the uncontrollable and therefore it's easier to get stuck with convictions that the egoic identity wants us to believe. To achieve intuitive living you don't need to change your circumstances or run away from what we would call hurdles or problems. It allows us to handle every situation with conscious decisions that lead to the best. There are always only solutions left. Always.

This multiverse is a place of constant expansion and evolution. If there is a problem, evolution finds a solution or transformation. We cannot run away from it, we don't need to run away, nor do we need to run faster to arrive. Evolution happens constantly in every given moment. Presence allows you to feel that flow of constant perfection in everything that is. We are not only the children of the stars, we are the stars and the creator of all the romantic told about them. Allow yourself now to arrive wherever you are. Take a look around you, see what is reality, see what is actually happening without any labelling. Just recognise, acknowledge and flow within it. This is a gift with which intuition blesses us all. Abundant love that's constantly demonstrated by us. If I press 'mycellf' down I as well do it with others, but if I recognise it I get the choice to liberate me and others from the casting of down pulling. I always think it is a beautiful way to make life more romantic understanding the habits that our cells are expressing, even though I feel there is a space between that, that leaves me with freedom of my individual intuitive expression of self. That is beyond what intellectual knowledge that I gain can understand. It is flowing beyond beliefs and convictions. Intuition teaches us about the concept of connection and disconnection. Nature inspires me always to better understand what I experience by this source of wisdom. Often it is as well the simple world around me that gives me examples on how love, peace and freedom can look.

Water of a spring never stops to flow because it doesn't like who's drinking it, air gives life to many beings and doesn't ask anything in return, the sun shines and just is; the sun allows all of us to experience light and in the evening the sun is so kind as to introduce us to the moon and the vastness of space. Did you ever see an apple tree that told you you're not worth it, not beautiful enough, not smart enough to pick it? Probably not, because nature provides us love and kindness without expectations. You feel the gratefulness entering your heart perceiving life through intuition? That's not only a thought; this is a thought, feeling and experience that's given to you to see beauty all around you and live a life in grace. It's a present, the only present that you have in every given moment. If you just cultivate intuition to this great gift that being alive is, getting the chance to live life like you were a newborn, then you will have spent this moment in love. Look around you; see how things are constantly changing, every moment everything is new. Can you find something right now that has changed in the last second? Living intuitively, we get the chance every moment to live through the eyes of a child, full of curiosity and joy.

A quiet mind is one which nothing weighs on, nothing worries, which, free from ties and from all self-seeking, is wholly merged into the will of God and dead to its own.

God wants nothing of you but the gift of a peaceful heart

—Meister Eckhart.

# 38. Experiencing All That Is

Take three deep breaths.

Arrive in the moment.

Do a body scan.

Now pay attention on which sense you're perceiving first: auditory, visual, smell, feeling on your skin or maybe taste.

Now pay real attention on this very sense.

Expand it and connect now to all senses at the same time: auditory, visual, smell, feeling on your skin and taste.

Feel them all in the same quality and presence.

Stay focused to give them all equal attention.

Feel how it feels to be totally aware of what reality is. No labelling, just be the perceiver. No action, just be there observing and perceiving all of your senses in the same moment. Allow yourself to see all the different nuances that each sense gifts you with. Be present for yourself and all that is. Invite yourself to be, just be, now.

Take a few moments to reflect on how you are feeling, how you experience and how you react to all that you perceive.

Thoughts create emotions, emotions are just hormones.

To know yourself as the Being underneath the thinker, the stillness underneath the mental noise, the love and joy underneath the pain, is freedom, salvation, enlightenment

—Eckhart Tolle

# 39.  Stress

If we don't live intuitively our world is shaped through various stressful conditions. The always negative downwards spiral leads the body to constant stress and degeneration. Those thoughts that are shaped by our beliefs change the serum level of many hormones including thyroid hormones, cortisol, growth hormones and prolactin. So in physically dangerous situations those serum level changes are genetically programmed for a so-called dangerous situation to be able to react quickly to protect oneself. Do you remember about the hormonal system alias endocrine system? So the endocrine system is not only challenged after being exposed to substances that lead to degeneration or disruption. Actually the endocrine system is as well disrupted in the same or even more intense way by stressful experiences and negative thoughts. Stress alters the natural healthy order of the endocrine system.

What is stress? Stress could be defined as any experience or moment which has the power to disturb or disrupt the harmony or as we would say the equilibrium between any living entity or organism and its environment. A life that's only led by convictions and beliefs on what we have to do, should do, still haven't done leads to stressful situations. Other reasons can be traumas that have not been metabolised or transformed yet. If you recognise that you have situations which seem very stressful I invite you to take a closer look on how to create a more aware state when stress is interrupting your natural energetic flow. If you recognise it you're already looking at it from an external perspective and can access your intuition immediately.

Your intuition always wants you to be in peace and everyone else around you as well. So what creates stress which then is a disruptor? There can be a variety of reasons. It could be stress of work pressure, examinations, psychosocial stress and physical stresses due to trauma, surgery and various medical disorders. I want to mention here that stress changes the levels of various hormones in our body. That's why in a stress situation we can have such an intense variety of sensations as well. This stress that occupies our physiology could be leading to various endocrine disorders.

So if we are constantly in stress and don't get the chance to metabolise it, it manifests itself in our cells and our energetic fields. This is just another invitation to take time during your daily life and unpractise the beliefs.

Unpractising is the only gate to see reality and allow yourself to get freedom of mind, health and peace. Live from within you, trust your heart and life will be space to create miracles every day.

How do I engage with my intuition in a stressful environment? With the most simple task which we just too often forget. Invite the own self back into itself. Take a deep breath, look what is happening around you in this very moment that you experience. Utilise the power of your two eyes. Eyes can see soul in any entity or object by just looking without labelling. Look at it without any labels, judgements or expectations. Breathe deeply. Connect to your breath and breathe yourself back into yourself. Only this moment is the gate to experience what is. It is the gate to stop fighting with reality and receiving reality the way it really is. Eyes may be a deep connection to know the other person without knowing them. It just happens as an exchange of presence. Whenever you look without the need to know you will know what is beyond the unknown.

Free choice is gained through intuition and all that happens will be an opportunity to learn how to deal with every outcome, whether physiological or emotional.

# 40.  Am I This Emotion?

We are all connected, not only through the five senses, but through the sixth and others. This allows us not only to feel our personal current state but it gives us the opportunity to feel what others feel and experience. If I take attention in a moment where I'm maybe overly euphoric or on the opposite side stressed, I can realise what is mine and what is from the external realm, like from strangers, friends or from my family, and then invite it to be experienced. All that I feel, think and experience doesn't need to be always created because of this individual incarnation. It can come from my energetic and cellular connection to my ancestors. It only appears that we are actually separated. But we are all connected through many layers and realms, through the physical and the not physically manifested. We carry the wisdom and experiences from our ancestors and the collective within us on a cellular level.

The biochemical structure, or better said, the biochemisty of the human body, becomes alive through our awareness. One could say it gets shaped by what we think and believe. All that we think about and what we have beliefs about can become our physiological biochemistry. Can you recall 'Thoughts create emotions, emotions are just hormones'? Actually every cellular structure within the human physiology is intuitive. It knows what its purpose is. Our cells listen to our thoughts, hear our words, they understand the intentions and are aware of our experiences. When I believe that my body is decaying and I'm ageing I age and decay faster than my intuitive cellular wisdom would have planned it. The mind has such power and the word is the intention that fires it to move. If you believe that you are old, sick, impatient, have a stressful life, no calm moment, your cells will believe it. You will manifest the word. If you on the other hand believe that you are healthy, young and have a vital, happy life, your cells will believe it. Your mind will be the mirror to your physiological expression. All those beliefs are safe within the genes and can be given further to children as well. Our beliefs provide the script to write or rewrite the code of our reality with a mind that's open and inspired to live whatever might come. Please notice that to be able to metabolise them all beliefs and thoughts may be integrated as they are a part of the human experience.

Out beyond ideas of wrongdoing
and rightdoing there is a field.
I'll meet you there.
When the soul lies down in that grass
the world is too full to talk about

—Rumi

Sometimes when we have difficult moments we would love to get a connection that is more touchy. Intuitive living gives us the opportunity to realise that those are just expectations that we programmed ourselves. If you go deep you stay connected to your intuition; you can sense, see, maybe feel or hear that we are always connected and always have the chance to get in connection in the physical world. Maybe you find a moment where you felt drawn to do or express your intuitive needs but your beliefs covered it up and you didn't take the chance. But even if we do not connect all the time in a physical, touchy way we are always surrounded by non-physical manifested forms as well.

I would love you to take a moment and reflect on it.

Where are other parts in your life where you connect and don't recognise it yet?

Can you see that you and me are connecting through this book right now? Why I'm making you aware of it is not to calm the part of you that feels disconnected, or take away the romanticism of being in touch with someone. It's to invite you to recognise the feeling of disconnection whenever it arises as an opportunity to allow yourself to just experience it without having the need to label it as beneficial or not beneficial on the concept of connection. Through just experiencing it you enter into a state where you're guided by your intuition that shows you what reality is.

Life will give you whatever experience is most helpful for the evolution of your consciousness. How do you know this is the experience you need? Because this is the experience you are having at the moment

—Eckhart Tolle (A New Earth: Awakening To Your Life's Purpose)

# 41. Feeding Self Roles and the Loss Of Intuition

Every thought and every emotion if they are not invited can lead to a physical and mental manifestation such as any kind of illness or condition. Intuition allows you to recognise it and just by allowing yourself to feel it and invite it you bring all of them into presence. Presence is the space where no suffering is left. Mostly those manifestations or imprints carry a personal experience with them. Now consider that in the beginning was the word and where you sent your attention energy starts to flow. Each time you travel to a moment where you identify with the story, either on your own or with a friend repeating over and over again the story, you get the opportunity and just judge the situation without fully inviting it. Then it manifests in the body. Every thought is a form of energy. Through intuition you can recognise which thoughts carry judgements and convictions and which just arise to open a space to get more freedom and peace.

How to get intuitive when you're stuck with your thoughts and emotions? Invite yourself to experience them like they would be your best friend. Just experience it within you. Maybe an event has happened to you. But recognise that what you're experiencing while thinking about it is just imagination. The egoic identity loves to feed on stories from the past to identify with the physical form and the imaginary form. It loves to share moments where it can feed from or maybe even get into that victim role related to an event. As cells in our body save all that we experience there can be times that those stories aren't processed in the same moment; as you live intuitively the physical manifestation of them can still be present and be used as a source of wisdom.

Recognise here what is really present in this very moment and what is a remembrance and image in your mind from maybe a couple of days, years, months or moments ago. So open your heart; you will invite those moments and see that they cannot harm you anymore. Those are just imaginary stories that are not happening right in front of your two eyes. They are not reality, they are a movie passing in the mind. The only thing you really have to do is connect to your intuition and be in this moment and let this sink in. This will open your energetic bodies and life can flow through you like clear water flows.

That doesn't mean that intuition keeps moments away from you that are not considered as beautiful. It allows you to shine light on what really is then we can release those stored energies and life can flourish. Negative thoughts and pain are teachers and pointers to make us aware to arrive in the present moment. When we are suffering in any sense our manifestation is telling us, 'Hey, you're right where you belong right now, come back and go deeper within you.' It's a great gateway to experience how each individual body works and a gate to heal traumata and unleash all energy in the body. To let go of the past and to let go of future expectations.

Suffering is an invitation to learn that the body is the temple of God, Tao or the universe, however you wish to call it. It flows through everything. It is the source that wakes us all up. We realise pain is only temporary and as well life in this physical form is. The soul never dies; living from intuition we can see that the soul is immortal and that it never dies. There is no such thing as death. There is only transformation of energy and manifestation. Death of this physical vehicle is fusion of one's manifestation with Mother Earth and all that resides here. It is becoming earth, water, air and fire. It is becoming all plants, all animals and all non-manifested. It becomes all, to become individual out of all and so on. It is learning each individuality and seeing similarities. It is the guide to empathy.

'You shall have no other gods before me.'

'You shall not make for yourself a carved image, or any likeness of anything that is in heaven above, or that is in the earth beneath, or that is in the water under the earth. You shall not bow down to them or serve them, for I the Lord your God and only worthy of worship, visiting the iniquity of the fathers on the children to the third and the fourth generation of those who hate me, but showing steadfast love to thousands of those who love me and keep my commandments.'

'You shall not take the name of the Lord your God in vain, for the Lord will not hold him guiltless who takes his name in vain.

'Remember the Sabbath day, to keep it holy. Six days you shall labor, and do all your work, but the seventh day is a Sabbath to the Lord your God. On it you shall not do any work, you, or your son, or your daughter, or your servant, or your livestock, or the sojourner who is within your gates. For in six days the Lord made heaven and earth, the sea, and all that is in them, and rested on the seventh day. Therefore the Lord blessed the Sabbath day and made it holy.'

'Honor your father and your mother, that your days may be long in the land that the Lord your God is giving you.'

'You shall not murder.'

'You shall not commit adultery.'

'You shall not steal.'

'You shall not bear false witness against your neighbor.'

'You shall not covet your neighbor's house; you shall not covet your neighbor's wife, or his male servant, or his female servant, or his ox, or his donkey, or anything that is your neighbor's.'

—Exodus 20:2-17 ESV; The Holy Bible

Empathy entails the ability to share feelings with other people. The downside can be empathic distress, which occurs when we imagine and internalise someone's pain. There are certain differences between empathic distress and compassion. In empathy, there are negative effects and activation of the anterior insula and the anterior cingulated cortex, a vital network of neurons that underlies empathy for pain. The main pain of empaths is the pain of others and to learn to distinguish between empathy and compassion. If we now look from empathy to the other hand, which would be compassion, there is activation of neuronal activity in the medial orbitofrontal, putamen, cortex, ventral tegmental area and pallidum which helps us to understand the other, be able to intellectualise the other's pain without suffering ourselves in a way that would harm our physiology. Which means simply said we will be compassionate. In addition, compassion is characterised by a warm state of positivity rather than a negative distressing state that is linked to empathy.

## 42. Stress, Fear, Trauma, Response and the Amygdala Hijack

There can be many instances, even not having a real threat, when humans are faced with extreme stress or fear. Often even trauma that couldn't be metabolised. According to one's beliefs then actions are guided by extreme emotions. So to explain it very simply, emotions are hormones and physiological reactions. Those signals can be experienced as something very threatening. In the body the first organ to receive a sensory stimulus which can create such a reaction is the thalamus. Part of the stimuli in thalamus goes to the neocortex (rational brain) and part goes to the amygdala (emotional brain). In the case of an experience of fear or stress, the amygdala triggers the HPA axis, so hijacking the neocortex. This is referred to as amygdala hijack. It results in the emotional brain activity occurring first before the rational brain activity. A side note here: the amygdala is as well a role player in processing the neuropeptide oxytocin, or better said, the often-called love hormone has the power to influence prosocial, generous and magnanimous decisions via the amygdala. That is what I sense utilising the mind as the source for forgiveness and peace. If it is the mind that creates one side it as well creates the opposite and most importantly what is beyond it.

... forgive them, for they do not know
what they are doing

—Luke Bible

Living from my intuition is being in meditation with all that comes. Increase in meditation helps to increase the connection between the rational brain and irrational brain so preventing the likelihood of an immediate emotional reaction when one experiences stress or fear. This occurs through activation of the prefrontal cortex and its linkage to the limbic system. The prefrontal cortex is responsible for the higher functions and it is commonly called the rational brain. The limbic system is responsible for the emotions. Hence, when one meditates, the linkage between these two helps in ensuring actions and emotions are dependent on each other and one does not act simply due to emotions. One usually acts in an irrational manner due to the sympathetic nervous system.

The sympathetic nervous system is responsible for the fight-and-flight response that is experienced in the likelihood of danger. It's not only what I sense with people that I get the chance to connect that cellfulness being within myself, inviting myself to change the way the mind and body functions but yes, there is research on meditation which indicates that the experience of meditation is linked with the structural and functional changes that are associated with decreased wandering of the mind. It as well supports the fact that meditation enhances physical and mental health. When I allow myself to arrive within me and metabolise what I experience I become me. Often I get the question, how do you do that people just feel so warm around you and where does this power of healing others come from?

First thing is making myself unpractise my beliefs and meditate on the moment. I never actually use the word healer and I want to mention here and show that it is not the other that is healing but what I do is be a guide to instruct how to heal as I walked this path in many ways already and know the shortcuts and the obstacles that may be there. What I even know more that all ways lead to Rome which is how my granny would say it. This neuroplasticity is what I feel changed within me after my later experience. I feel rewired. Reconnected to a deeper wisdom. All that I tell you here shall be a guide to use the intellect as a friend and open space for not being who we think we are. If I become aware of my inner states I learn how to cope with emotions and distinguish between the perceived reality and what is really happening.

How is neuroplasticity relevant to all my emotional intelligence and self-reflection?

As we've seen, neuroplasticity means that our brain changes in response to our experience and this you will experience with all the practices within this book. This means that we unintentionally change our brain all of the time just by changing what we pay attention to and what our habits are. The good news is, this means also that we can intentionally change our brain by choosing where to direct our attention. Not only the brain actually but yes, the knowledge of the whole body. Practising and including the beautiful tools that science reveals to support us integrate what we have left apart about ourselves and is crucial for a holistic life. I primarily was introduced to meditation studies by my friends Tottie Yokota and Miguel Mayher from mayher.org which led me to pay attention to a beautiful project developed at Google by leading experts in neuroscience, business and psychology which is called Search Inside Yourself and has the the beautiful title 'The Unexpected Path to Achieving Success, Happiness and World Peace'. When they introduced me to mindfulness and emotional intelligence I just felt immediately drawn to know more about it. It showed me scientific explanations on how I experience life. So to come to the point, it is attention that gives us the power to love life and as well the downside.

Now, choosing where to direct our attention in a way that nourishes our cells unfortunately does often not come naturally. Most of us have not learnt what that even means. At least I didn't. There are more distractors that consume our attention every day. Fortunately, looking from a scientific point of view, there are tools to train our ability to choose where to direct our attention such as self-reflection, meditation, mindfulness, journaling and other awareness practices. All of these are the base to better understand the wisdom of intuition.

And yes, like we all know, where attention goes, energy flows.

The practice of living intuitively changes the wires in our brain. It 'unwires' our beliefs and rewires us for reality. It takes old wires, transforms them and clears all that we have accumulated. Those accumulations that work as filters do not only filter away reality. They filter what is good for our cells and keep away what nourishes us. The soul itself expresses its intuitive wishes while we find the balance and the unbalance and integrate it all. It is the integration of oneself to the physical dimension. It is the opportunity to live here on the planet with an open heart and full consciousness. It allows me to look beyond the concept of physical matter. Beyond physical appearance and behaviour. All manifested matter consists of neutrons, electrons and protons if we would break it down. Intuition integrates it without any breakdown. It allows seeing that the form we have comes from the same source. It even shows what is beyond the tallest structure that exists and leads to the source of existence. I reveal myself to consist the same way out of neutrons, electrons and protons. I reveal that the consciousness behind it is my revelation. One does not reveal itself without the other. It is the mirror of unacceptance and acceptance. All that I converted will once be converted into the other.

For love I come to you without me, for love you
come to me without you

—Rumi

Intuition supports me finding the right questions for myself for my cells and using the intellect to get deeper into the experience of intuition. It allows me to inspire humans from different places with different beliefs and convictions. It allows me to inspire myself to see reality and experience oneness.

Language is here a skill to open the doors that lead to what's hidden behind beliefs. 'In the beginning was the word.'

Neuroscience is the opportunity to understand better how the vehicle that we reside in functions. As well understanding from neurobiology how not only our habits, beliefs and autopilot states interact with our experience but yes, all other that we ingest into our body. Knowing the body and seeing the total experience as a holistic one. It can be seen as a resident in a new house experiencing how to handle the house and where the hidden spots and beauties are. So neuroscience helps us to provide scientific knowledge to compare us and show that actually intuition and science are twins. As you might have noticed all that is written here is an intellectual way to invite yourself to experiential.

If I allow myself to 'unpractise' the constant need for compulsive behaviour and follow deeper the intuitive wisdom I create peace. Seeing life as a mirror and living intuitively has the power to get deeper into the state of flow, creativity, compassion and productivity.

# 43. 'Cellfulness'

Mystics, scientists and philosophers have long
researched how to achieve a state of clear mind and tried
to figure out if we can change our thought and belief
structures. Also called Mindfulness. The question is, can
you rewire your brain to get out of a constant
downwards spiral of thinking? The answer is yes, you
can. We know that it is practice that leads to non-
practice. Or sometimes suffering that leads to clarity,
and clarity that leads us to see the suffering.

In the previous part of the book I explained how
valuable it is to be in a state where all flows to
unpractise and arrive in the moment. We have seen
reasons that can make the physiological experience more
agreeable and what may be reasons that we aren't feeling
ourselves in joy. With simple attention in the inner body
and for what really happens in the outer world we are
able to break away from limiting thought patterns. This
does not mean you're going to be forced with attention
in your body. Take the practice of being in the moment

as a joyful opportunity to gain your lovely, curious and adorable childish side back. It allows you to break all limiting thought patterns and karmic beliefs that are often almost like regions, and open the opportunity to be born new every moment. Any practice where you allow yourself to totally engage relaxes the limiting mental constraints and supports you to break through old accumulated habits and rewire your brain and change its structure.


I would like to elaborate on what being 'cellfull' is for me. It is the practice of achieving a life with awareness of the way the cells interact with the world around us. It's the simple, gainable ability to see what is happening in your body, mind and environment without being totally identified with it. Body and mind are always one, thus for intellectual understanding I've chosen to speak about each. A great example is traffic: how do you react if you get cut by another car? Our convictions make us judgemental and as we know the egoic identity loves to fight with reality. Why the other driver really has 'cut' you doesn't matter for the egoic identity, it just wants to show how upset it is. So what happens next is the reaction to the emotion that's created through expectations of how that other person should have acted and invite only those expectations into your cells instead of letting the intuitive wisdom flood your 'cellf'. The egoic identity loves to identify with the thought of being upset because of the other driver and react to the belief of how it should have been reacted. These emotions are mostly only expressed to the external world and not experienced in the internal, so they would manifest in the physical body, such as getting stored as a short traumatic stress which leads to blockages of our energetic flow. What you think is what you become.

Our beautiful human brain is as well the central organ for the stress response that we experience. It tells us what stressful means. More interesting, I find that the brain is also on attack I would say from stress and it then changes the structure and chemistry. Here it doesn't matter if it is just a little stress or constant, or better said, chronic stress.

So by identifying with a thought pattern or an image in our mind about ourselves immediately we lose the ability to reflect on the present moment. The egoic identity gets into a story and the mind wanders to the past and can't see that the moment is already gone. In the egoic or identified mind there is compassion and empathy only for selected entities that fit into the current created identity theme. No way to understand the other. If we learned to create a short time buffer between thought and reaction to experience the energy of this moment and invite it to see reality, that's when I would invite myself into my 'cellfs' and create a state where I'm inside my cells. With a little bit of actively being 'cellfull' you can start to recognise where the energy gets blocked. Maybe in your lungs, maybe your heart is buzzing, maybe you start to shake in the hand, your face is turning red, you get thoughts about who is right in this situation. The term 'cellfullness' is having a cell full with one's attention. So could this full cell support to achieve an intuitive approach? With cellful, I mean a moment to be totally present in the now, connecting to intuition and inviting yourself to 'yourcellf.'

So often I speak about listening to the cells and looking if they get closed or opened as a reminder if it is intuition speaking. There is the question, is it ever justified to get angry? Do I ever need to get angry? Remember, living intuitively is not about ignoring your feelings, it's an opportunity to invite them to understand them, and from this show your thoughts where peace comes from. It comes from a natural state of flow that doesn't judge you nor the thoughts of others. It doesn't mean you need to be in a state that doesn't have any intuitive judgements anymore; it's more a way of being released of those energies that we store in our body without being aware of it. Being intuitive and practising 'cellfulness' is learning how to respond with inner wisdom to any given circumstances rather than just reacting in rage.

So how to get into cellfulness practice? Any of the practices that I mention in this book are gateways to an expanded perceivable connection between what is that your cells want to express and what is imagination. I've learned that there is only one way to live in peace and this is through living intuitively. So can cellfulness be a practice to start living more intuitive? Yes.

If you have reflected on your time on Earth, you might recognise that our beliefs make us not see the reality and facts. Through evolution nature gave us the ability to be constantly judging everything to be sure to survive from experiences of natural threats, wars and social interventions that can turn not only into physical violence, it as well enhances emotional and conversational violence. Most decisions that are taken to get into a state of suffering or make others suffer come from emotions that are created through our beliefs. Remember that thoughts create emotions and emotions are the expression of hormones that we are able to sense what is currently happening in our belief system and our surroundings. If we believe what we think we become what we believe.

All emotions are essential features of normal human experience. So as mentioned, some of the most emotional and traumatic conditions involve emotional disorders that arise through beliefs that do not allow us to look beyond the sphere that's created through identity. In this physical body we have survival instincts that don't necessarily help us to see reality as it is in a neutral, caring and loving way, but only if those instincts are imaginarily triggered rather than by the reality. Intuition is here the key to open those locked beliefs and traumas to be able to see that there is so much miracle on this planet. Through programmed or behaviour systems that we accumulate through imitating not only our parents, teachers, friends till the middle age, and then get the opportunity to create a fixed self-image on who we are cages us in an imaginary world.

The egoic identity loves to identify with its own story and as well loves when others strengthen this story to feel righteous about the personal beliefs. From a tribal perspective that might be the most logical way to stay connected with the ideological beliefs. Those beliefs are as well the opportunity to create social alienation and segregation which leads to disconnection. Intuition on the other hand allows us to clear all those ideological beliefs and live from the individual inner source of wisdom where no borders exist between race, nationality, ethnicity, or religious and political tribes; it is lived altruism without the belief that altruism should exist. It helps us to understand others and create empathy. Naturally everyone you meet, see and think about will be a portal for you to enter deeper in reality. It gifts you with the power of blowing up chains for a world where borders will be used only for practical reasons.

Coming back to the way the egoic identity acts when a belief is not met, it actually loves always to fight and therefore it prefers to disagree and isolate itself and others if they do not fit in the current belief system of how they should be and act. As you know in the beginning was the word, and the word creates our world.

The word can be seen here as our beliefs and the world as our physical expression.

Let's see what beliefs are and how they interact with the way that we perceive things. So probably we all have a sense of what beliefs are; let's look a little deeper to see the interaction that they have with our biology. A belief can actually be seen as the conceptual guiding principle in life that can provide directions and even meaning. Beliefs are filters which organise our behaviour and shape our perception of what we think our inner and the external world is like. They work like an inner commander to demand and make us act according to what we believe to be true.

What often happens if we don't have conceptual beliefs is that we can feel disempowered. Most convictions and beliefs originate from what we have experienced with our senses, from hearing and seeing, mostly from others since childhood.

Beliefs are shaped through our external world like the environment we live in, religious beliefs, cultural beliefs, experiences and events, accumulated knowledge, imagination... Can we change those beliefs? Even ones that are burned into our cells through traumatic experiences? Yes. I have learned that any belief can be transformed. Do we have the power to actually choose what we believe in? We do and even more romantically beautiful I find is that they become what we think reality is. Beliefs are not just unpractical and unneeded patterns, but are crucial for our romanticism. They are woven into our experience of emotions being aware or unaware of those. We go in symbiosis with them and that's why the egoic identity feels threatened to die and often even can be expressed in aggression. All rooted when the individual beliefs are challenged.

Often we would think that our beliefs which trigger our emotional brain is only local in the hippocampus, amygdala and hypothalamus. But being aware of the placebo and nocebo let us see that beliefs don't only manifest in the brain but as well in the rest of our physiology. In biomedical history it's noticed that placebos have a tremendous, profound effect on a variety of conditions and disorders. What I found was one astounding case where a woman was suffering from severe nausea and vomiting. What I understood was while measuring the gastric contractions her complaints were matching those disrupted patterns that were measured. So the scientists introduced a new magical, extremely potent drug which would, the doctors proclaimed, undoubtedly cure her nausea. The amazing thing was within a couple of minutes, her nausea was cured.

Funnily, the exact same gastric tests now revealed that there was no disturbed pattern but yes, normal patterns. But actually what she had been given was the syrup of ipecac. So syrup of ipecac is a substance that is usually used to induce nausea! That's the power that our beliefs behold. So after when the syrup was shown to her, combined with the suggestion of relief of nausea she was suffering from, by a person she had believed to be an authority figure, it worked like a command to the brain that triggered an orchestra of self-regulatory biochemical responses within her body. It wasn't the first time the placebo showed the power of belief. But an important one to recognise in biomedical research that a placebo can be a more potent drug than even 'believed'.

What seems important in the observation of this patient is that the placebo response seemed to involve the meaning of the disorder for her as well as the illness itself to her individual beliefs. Broken down, a person's belief and the interpretation instantaneously can govern biological responses or behaviours. Interesting, isn't it? Something else I found was about a schizophrenic woman who was observed to have split personalities. So under normal conditions when she would feel fine, her blood glucose levels were normal. However, the moment she believed she was diabetic, her entire physiology changed to become that of a diabetic, including elevated blood glucose levels. Every time I remind myself about that I get amazed by the power of our convictions and beliefs.

I would like to elaborate on something from the daily life here. Once I visited a lovely lady close to my home town. She wasn't feeling very fit so we spoke about how to increase the intuitive wisdom to have whatever might be the best for her physiology. I sensed that there was more that hadn't been shared. I could see it in her voice and thought that there was something locked. I asked her if there was something she didn't feel that she could express with her voice. So indeed, she wasn't able to sing anymore. A couple of years ago she had lost her voice. Since then she never sang again. I felt how on one side she wanted so much to sing again and on the other hand there was the identification with the story of the big trauma that happened and she carried it around. A big sense of self was deriving from that traumatic moment. She went to lots of doctors to try to cure it but since that day she even lost the belief that she still could sing. While she was sharing this intimate experience with me I felt that there was still a part left in her that believed she could sing. It was just under that loud mental voice and as well within her environment. Everyone knew she had lost her voice and everyone gave her sympathy and felt sorry for her. She told me that she gave up singing forever. When she said that we both knew that this information wasn't coming from her intuition. I asked her if she believed that if her intuition wants her to be in peace if an answer with such an heavy weight would come from her intuition? She said no. So I asked her who does she want to believe in, her imagination or her intuition? She said her intuition. She said from now on every time she thinks she can't sing she will listen to her inner voice. Since that day on she started again to sing in band and jam sessions. I met her a couple of months ago; she told me that she hasn't been feeling more free since her childhood. What I want to show here is that sometimes our convictions can hold us from just taking even the step and metabolise the past. Trauma creates often such a strong belief which can shape the way we think reality is. And it shapes it so dramatically well that reality seems absurd.

Take a moment and reflect on what I shared with you here. In the beginning was the word. This is so powerful that I can't express how I feel saying these six words. Here I invite you again with all of my heart to have an open mind and heart to enjoy your intuition and learn what your personal and individual placebo is. Living intuitively we integrate our beliefs and evolve with them. We keep those who are beneficial but don't identify with them anymore. They become like a friend that we can invite into our temple or not. In a world where we all live intuitively there is no space left for segregation. We naturally connect with love, health, freedom and peace and spread it to everyone around us. Being able to see your individual placebos can release them or strengthen you in situations that you might benefit from them. Understanding what to surrender to and which belief works and intellectually benefits you in this very moment helps to understand and see how the complexity of each individual is expressed. Looking beyond beliefs is seeing reality.

There is actually a backfire effect when something contradicts with our existing beliefs and convictions.

The egoic identity becomes more convinced that this belief is the only reality and judge others if they do not agree. Judging others or fighting against their beliefs is like throwing oil into fire. This actually creates a lack of empathy and compassion on both sides. When humans get divided into separate groups they instinctively become less empathetic because the egoic identity gets the opportunity to identify itself with a reinforcing belief system from the group. Instinctively means for the sake of the survival of the egoic identity we connect less to other races, religions and even other sports teams. This is a main factor that empathises racism, slavery and genocide in society. Only an intuitive approach that comes from a space of empathy and compassion leads us to a peaceful outcome.

Do you have any belief that makes you feel that there is a group that you don't belong to, or a group that does not belong to your group? I invite you to go deeper and let this sink in through the 10 questions of intuition.

If you would like actively to practise intuitive living with others and open your and others' perspectives, it's important to respond empathically. Connect to your inner source, find what it is that you both or maybe a whole group has in common and connect through that. Your intuition will lead you to see what connects you that's beyond caging beliefs. This will dis-identify the belief of the opposite side and the personal egoic convictions and no longer be seen as a threat. It will allow you to see that we are sitting all in the same boat here on this beautiful planet. So you will recognise that you can enter into a state of connectedness or directly through the non-practice of intuition or the practice itself where you integrate the other into your beliefs and see them the way they really are. See reality.

Let's do a little eight-step practice.

Please take a moment to reflect which groups you recognise that you would not feel comfortable joining and maybe even have a feeling that they don't have anything in common with your life.

Step 1. Write down what it is that those people do that you recognise as a behaviour that should not have been expressed. Write down three examples.

Step 2. Now please write down three advices for them of how they should instead behave.

Step 3. Please write down things that the people from this group and you have in common. Three examples.

(Notice that there are no rules, you can write whatever comes in your mind reading those steps but keep the answers within the question.)

Step 4. Please write down what experiences you might have in common with these group 3 examples.

Step 5. Please go now to Step 2. And take those advices to turn them around and see them as a mirror. Each of the three examples. Write them down as an advice to yourself. For example, if you wrote the person should … then turn it into, I should...

Step 6. Write down three examples where it would be that you should take those three advices …

Step 7. Go to Step 1 and take those three behaviours to turn them around and see them as a mirror. Each of the three behaviours. Write them down as if you would have those behaviours towards yourself or others. For example, if you wrote the person behaves … or the person is... then turn it into, I am … I behave …

Step 8. Take a moment and reread it and see where it is that your external world mirrors your behaviour.

There is nothing in this world that is not a source of wisdom and every step can be one towards the other which is always one towards myself as well. Only by inviting myself into my cells is it when I metabolise my beliefs and turn them into a pointer to reality.

We are humans, we breathe the same air, we drink from the water that Mother Earth provides, we eat the fruits that trees gift to us … Allow yourself to always integrate that you can be wrong, because the mind always loves to fight with reality. Allow and express to others that is okay to be 'wrong' even if there is no real wrong, it is just a clustered belief that can't look further than the convictions. So invite your thoughts, your convictions and your beliefs to be nourished by the freeing wisdom of intuition. All that we experience is an opportunity to reflect on ourselves and the way the world around us is created.

Sometimes we align because we have similar experiences and perspectives, sometimes because we have similar values and agree on a lot, sometimes because we feel we carry the same energy and sometimes because we just see the human in front of us for what he is in this very moment.

Living intuitively is training the mind to be rewired to experience joy of being whenever I'm with myself or with someone else. I've learned that even the smallest things can enlighten our cells and change the wires that cause the physical and emotional suffering. As long as you suffer you carry your karma; as soon as you invite your suffering and care of it free of judgements you arrive in the moment where the past has no power over you. The real power drives from the existing. Living intuitively is the option to consciously rewire the physical and energetic body to such an extent that there is no karma, no trauma and no darkness left. What is left is the integration of all of them and to use them as your wisdom source. It is the gate to be connected. Not for a few seconds, not for only some moments, not for only a couple of days. It is the practice that enlightens mind and body to practise beliefs.

We are the mirror, as well as the face in it.
We are tasting the taste of eternity this
minute.
We are pain and what cures pain.
We are the sweet cold water and the jar that
pours.
Soul of the world, no life, nor world remain,
no beautiful women and men longing.
Only this ancient love circling the holy black
stone of nothing.
Where the lover is the loved, the horizon and
everything within it

—Rumi

## 44. Intuition and Relational Expectations

Let me start here first with an example. A while ago I had a beautiful experience with a couple. Both just had accomplished two years of relationship and just moved into an apartment together. She had just found out that she was pregnant and he that he's going to be a father. This led them to learn to step back from their own self to now send the attention to the child that would be in couple of months their portal for a new way to experience life. Daily life and family can be the biggest challenge when it comes to live intuitively. Often we do not live from our source of wisdom but from our convictions that constantly try to convince us to compromise and lead us away from the intuition. So there was a conflict situation where it was from two sides.

From his side: You are never listening to me when I express my feelings.

From her side: You're not giving me attention and this leads to stress for me and the baby.

Recall the practice of the 10 Point Intuition Cell-Awareness Method to recognise intuition; you can use either the intellectual way through the questions to arrive in reality, or there is a beautiful technique to clear the egoic identity's need to righteousness and totally connect to the present moment, leaving the past behind.

This technique works best the way we've been created. Naked, no clothes and no jewellery. It is a practice in presence with oneself and another person.

Sit opposite each other, straight, on a chair. Close that you can easily grab each other's hand. On one side the man holds the hand on the bottom and on the other hand the woman holds on the bottom.

Take three deep breaths and look into each other's eyes without dodging.

Allow yourselves to just look into each other's eyes without looking away, without expressing anything, without saying anything; try not to blink a lot.

Just look at your partner's eyes and experience what it feels like.

Can you experience the space you are giving yourself and your partner to just be and experience the essence of the other?

Just look and appreciate this moment.

Right now, are you thinking about your own name?

About where your cellphone is?

About what your best friend might be doing?

Nope, that's right; you are experiencing looking into the eyes of your partner without the story that normally comes with it. You are looking at him through the eyes of a child.

Giving your full presence just by looking into each other's eyes, don't think about the past, nor the future. This is the opportunity to see beyond our beliefs how our partners are. This is the opportunity to see them as they are in this given moment.

Keep looking into each other's eyes a couple more minutes and experience how it feels to just be without labelling the partner. Feel the freedom that arises within you and the peace that comes with it.

This technique is an extremely powerful tool in relation to stopping acting with the partner, stopping the need to appear in a role, stopping practising and doing anything to change the other. This practice allows us to unpractise our beliefs and create freedom of mind and peace.

Genius is patience.

—Isaac Newton

Living intuitively is being genius.

How does that sound to you? How do you feel hearing that? I would love you to explore it.

Let me go into it. As you know, intuition is the opportunity to invite life because only then may I understand the individuality of how joy looks for me. Being a genius looks to be only available for a small group of people. But let me ask you in which field are you a genius?

Reflect on it and find one.

So what has intuition to do with being a genius? Let's start with elaborating on genius. Let me contemplate on how etymological perspectives handle genius. Short and precise. Genius from Latin is the guardian spirit of a person, the spirit, inclination, wit, genius and literally the inborn nature. From gignō it's correlated to beget and produce. In old Latin genō, from the Proto-Indo-European root, it relates to see, seeing. So reflect on that. If you look and intellectualise on all that we have learned here about intuition isn't that a fit that is not only for a small group of people but for every person, as we all have the guiding gift of intuition? Connecting to intuition allows us to not look at the things that separate us but yes, to look at what we have in common. It's being newborn and reincarnated within this given lifetime. It's being able to see and expand to be not only what we see to be the seen object and look back at us.

Then for the first time you look
around and the beauty of nature is
revealed. Then you listen to the
harmony of the universe, the
symphony of the stars. Then
everything starts to become more and
more beautiful. Layers and layers of
beauty are revealed. Your eyes have a
penetrating force. Wherever you look
you go deep. Even in rocks you feel
flowers blossoming

— Tao, The Three Treasures 4

In most relationships that aren't based on intuitive interactions—those could be with parents, partners or even children—we often tend to just fill a hole that we sense within us. But this hole can never be full, it's like a black hole transforming all energy into something else and even then humans don't feel fulfilled. The egoic identity loves to search for all that we already have. It loves to lose what is given and take what is lost. It's like its main goal is to separate from a 3-D perspective even if there is no such thing as separation. If love turns to fear or hate or appreciation into segregation it wasn't love that has taken place, it was just the idea of love. Love is borderless. Love has no borders regarding behaviour, beliefs, actions, ethics or attitudes. It can be perceived as love from the egoic identity where it actually is a form of limitation, alienation and separation. The way I see love it actually has no opposite; maybe Hollywood love, yes. I sense love as something that's more formless than the belief on what love does and how it has to make me feel. When I'm in love I feel freedom. So how can I ask any to love only love me and therefore take away the freedom that love has to offer? The egoic identity loves to fight with reality and therefore loses the opportunity to love who is and what is right in front of us. If there is no freedom for me letting my partner love whomever he wants then it might be an idea about love that I have.

Intuition here takes the role of a gentle teaching, pointing out what reality wants us to perceive. If you look around you may perceive again that what is just happening in this moment is reality and it is so much kinder than our imagination can lead us to believe.

In the beginning was the word. Words shape. Using words with the intention of peace and curiosity creates freedom, using words from my story can be shaping reality into imagination. It's a beautiful practice to be using words to let reality be as it is and turn from the labeller to the perceiver that holds the moment with gentle awareness.

It is God You Love
… Although you may not know it,
If you love anyone, it is Him you love;
If you turn your head in any direction,
It is towards Him you turn.

… In the light I praise you
and never knew it.
In the dark I slept with you
and never knew it.
I always thought that I was me,
But no, I was you
And never knew it

—The World's Wisdom

Fear of freedom is fear of love.

What fear am I speaking about here? It is the fear of letting the other do what he ever decides to do. It keeps us from living a free life and letting our beloved ones be free. It cages love into boxes. Believing that anyone should compromise is like a conviction that filters reality. It filters love and makes it into a role game on how someone should act or shouldn't. It's all about acting here. Control, cage or limit anyone. Love is beyond beliefs, beyond connection or disconnection; it is union with the universe. Looking deeper into couple goals which most of the time aren't what the heart is calling for we can dig deeper. What's behind all the compromises and all the rules and limitations of what the partner isn't allowed to do?

Intuition is telling you that the goal is peace, freedom of mind and health. So can that be achieved if we really try to limit ourselves and others by acting like in a role game? I'd love to invite you here to reflect and let those questions sink in.

Where do you ask your beloved one to compromise and don't compromise yourself?

Where do you ask your partner to keep what he has promised and don't hold a promise yourself?

Where is it that you need more love and caring and don't care nor love enough yourself?

In relationships we get constant free individual teachings from everyone that lives in a relationship with us. If we can't see that yet in a difficult relationship then we might not be ready to accept that. Can you recall the elaboration on emptiness? Which is often the cause of intellectual subconscious beliefs on how connection looks. So to fill that we look for something that fits our beliefs on what would fit in. So the piece that we think is missing we try to amplify through giving people and objects labels that we think could fill that emptiness that we experience. But we all know where attention goes energy flows. The belief that something is missing is like a self-fulfilling prophecy. In the beginning was the word. You remember the placebo and nocebo? It could be a good metaphor for this topic. We shape our reality with our beliefs. Remember, intuition is always showing us the kindness of reality; if we feel something is wrong or not right with a person or an object and judge it we give this belief the power to shape our lives.

Intuition is here the key point to distinguish between reality and beliefs and furthermore understand the personal beliefs and invite them with kindness. This invitation and acceptance of beliefs clears them, neutralises them and helps us unpractise our beliefs. Intuition helps to understand the individual needs of each personal expression of self on an emotional and physiological level. Gently remind yourself that both cannot be seen as separate, nor any relation we have with any entity. So whatever happens in the thoughts becomes a mirror in the external world.

So if I believe that someone or something will fulfill me because I subconsciously or consciously believe something is missing in me it leads me to believe that I don't have it within me, especially when it comes to love relations. If we look at it on the level of consumption, if I believe that food is my fuel but because of chemicals and soils that aren't rich in nutrients I can't be healthy I created a belief that shapes my reality.

Ask me what heals me, I will tell you I
don't know. I can't know.


If I'm not healed I'm not in love. Only
when I'm in love I know how to be
healed. Intuition is my portal to love.

# 45. Being in Love

Anybody who lives from their essence will not need to receive any gift in this world; thus anybody who lives from their essence will see the value of every gift. There is nothing to give and nothing to take if you hear the source of existence from within you. It will just flow. It is the realisation of the soul.

Looking deeper into what love is considered to be I found that it seems that love as an experience is deeply rooted in human biology. The romantic around the concept of love and as well the experience of borderless love is a coherent aspect of being human and has and still is an inspiration for any kind of art. Concept of love can start before entering in a relationship with a person or object or be created after the immediate experience of love when the mind tries to label it or make it fit into an inner or external belief system. Can you recall some moment where you felt the profound feelings and emotions that love or the absence of it can cause? The mental and physical state can alter from regeneration to degeneration. Did you ever hear someone tell a story about a person that couldn't live anymore or even died because of a broken heart? Even a failed relationship or a death of a beloved one can have disastrous physiological and psychological effects. This goes deeper than the basic needs. Without loving relationships we can't flourish and here it doesn't matter if all other basic needs are already met.

So love is not just an emotion. It indeed is as well a biological process. When we get the opportunity to spend a moment with someone that we love this activates our individual cognitive and physiological processes which then work as a reflection in our mental and as well emotional states. Whatever we experience may then shape the way we express ourselves in the future. It seems that love requires constant feedback, for example, just by mentally noticing someone is there for us or we can be there for someone and as well in a physiological behaviour of touching and stroking. The physiology of being a human seeks this experience of love and responds coherently to interaction with persons that are loved ones and as well, like mentioned above, when the absence of such interaction of love is present.

It seems as well that love does not come without danger. How does that sound to you? Often the way we respond to strong emotions which can be triggered by love might leave us vulnerable and more drawn to invite what we imagine the other has or hasn't said than what reality is.

From the concept of love failed relationships indeed have degenerative and deadly effects on our cells. Since the technology is increasing our ability to experience love as well increases in its vastness. It can happen that love functions through communication technology and social media by believing the concept of how love looks and in daily life maybe it even doesn't work. Interesting is that the risk for social isolation is a tremendous indicator for the body's autonomic nervous system to get into disorder, if we believe the convictions of the mind. This can include deficits in its capacity for social interactions and love itself. This is conceptual knowledge to support you to find concepts and allow intuition to look where it is love and freedom is guiding me and where a concept of love is that cages me. Here I would love you to reflect on the following questions. Note there is no right or wrong answer.

Let me ask you what kind of love that I described can be dangerous?

Do you think that love would make anybody suffer?

Think about a relationship of love that you have, are you creating anywhere in the relationship borders?

Is being emotional or vulnerable something that you feel uncomfortable with?

What is love for you?

All those questions are an opportunity to connect to your individual answers; it's an invitation to

Feel

Recognise

Have a non-judgemental attitude towards the feelings

Invite the answers as a friend.

# 46. 'Cellular Disorders' and the 'Disordered Mind'

What are cellular disorders? For me, they are actually similar to mental conditions which can affect how we experience emotions, affecting cognition and our behaviour. It happens when I don't have the opportunity into invite myself to myself or I'm having all my attention far away from my cellular wisdom. Not being within 'mycellf'. There are different gradations of mind that are disordered when I can't invite myself into mycellfs; this can go from states that are recognised as acute, or maybe even depression, anxiety and neurosis. It looks like any disorder of me not being able to invite myself and can hold back the intuitive wisdom the individual has to offer. If you recall, there are some physiological reasons and mental reasons why we may not be able to communicate with the cells and both have to do with the individual expression of self, what we received from our ancestors and what we collected in this life. Understanding that the individual self is the one self with all selfs. So your individual expression of self stems from the same source of existence as my individual expression of self.

Often physiological or mental conditions can be an individual expression of source wisdom which hasn't been seen as an opportunity to look deeper but as a condition to treat. There may be a physiological reason that may allow oneself to be considered the one with the mind that is disordered when I can't invite myself into mycellf or create thought patterns and have stuck traumatas in the cells. So generally a 'cellular disorder' and mind that's out of order can interfere with the ability to learn and interact within social life, sense what the body needs, interfere with the ability to communicate properly what our inner world would like to express in family and work life.

For me, the roots of disease are very deeply written into our cells. I don't see it as a condition but as something we can't understand yet and has a pointer to learn more about individuality. On the other hand, one can't say that a genocide isn't a mental condition; it is on the level of the third-dimensional thought, yes. And as well there is something deeper to learn out of it for the collective. Why does a mind that is disordered even evolve? There are many genetic and non-genetic risk factors but one reason is that the person wasn't able to have the chance to metabolise a traumatic psychological or traumatic physiological experience. So risks to 'be the one' with the mental condition can include high rates of attention deficit hyperactivity disorder. Disorders like autism and substance use disorders are as well included here. As well major depressive disorder and most anxiety disorders and eating disorders are considered in the range of mind that is disordered when I can't invite myself into mycellf.

I want to mention here that there is no such thing as being the one or having one with a mental condition or disorder as there is no one that doesn't learn from this interaction while being here on earth. What they all have in common is the physiology misses metabolising experiences and therefore misses reality. My intention here is to see that not being able to live in reality can cause lots of harm to the body and the mind and I know that in my life it was the suffering of it that led me to integrate this experience into the wholeness. Sometimes the cells carry those unmetabolised experiences for centuries with them and give them further to children and then there is an individual expression that starts to flower and spread the seeds of wisdom till the life has left the physiology. This is a very delicate topic and therefore I want to invite you to read with the heart rather than with the mind. So why I am including this?

Just to go back to the level of concepts and understand a little more about the physiology, do you remember the nocebo and placebo? Looking into psychiatry we now know that the placebo effect has a crucial role in most psychiatric conditions which include anxiety, addictions, depression, and contrary to what was expected even schizophrenia. So even in schizophrenia the knowledge about the condition would interfere with the expression of the condition. For a very long time research was focusing on the brain to understand neurobiological mechanisms of anxiety- and trauma-related disorders. For me, many of those disorders as well held the inflammation of the body within. It is for me a part of ascendance of body and mind. On one hand it is a physiological inflammation and a condition which as well is a fragmented truth. As unnecessary as it may sound suffering itself and any coming condition seems to be a part of unfolding and unfiltering the wisdom of the source of existence.

Every emotional state that is keeping us from living a healthy, fulfilled life could be seen as a psychiatric condition or mental illness. Too often emotional understanding is pushed away and just seen as something psychiatric. I have seen that its roots are the same biologically as any other condition or physiological illness. I rather would say that any state that I experience and can be still aware of can be a pointer to where I disorder my attention in my mind and body thus I know whenever I create a concept on what is health and disease for me I miss the wisdom that my intuition is telling me. So what is mental illness for me? It's the condition that the whole body including my beliefs can make me ill through my patterns, the not understanding of a spiritual experience and beliefs or any physiological reaction. Beyond this condition there

is a field that flows through every being on this world.
It's a form of consciousness that's within every object
and entity on this planet.

So would it be like the statement that mental illnesses
are similar to any other medical illness? Mental illnesses
indeed have a biological basis just like other medical
illnesses. Any experience of emotions, the speaking
mind and therefore thoughts, creates perception and the
way we take action according to this is shaping our
human identity patterns and the concept of oneself.
Often it can happen when one believes this person is
itself and oneself only that we create vaster
disconnection on the third level.

Any belief of segregation and alienation can besides
physiological traumas or expressions as well alter the
human physiology and then lead to a mind that is
disordered when I can't invite myself into mycellfs.

When I try to find out at the level of materialisation what
could be risk factors for a mind that is disordered when I
can't invite myself into mycellfs it is not only
consumption of what I think and inflames me or my
nutrition that could be high in inflammatory foods but it
goes from trauma to isolation and psychological
deprivation as well. They can have the root in a familiar
environment very often which then grows into work and

social life. Thus I know the deeper wisdom that this beholds will be expressed one day.

Finding reasons for a mental condition isn't so easy even if we go into psychologising it. The mind loves to find reasons and solutions and on a human level to use communication is a beautiful tool to integrate the intellect as a friend as well. What I sense and see is that if we create a dialogue about this delicate topic we may find something deeper hidden behind what we experience as mental condition, depression, anxiety or traumata than we conceptually may be able to grasp. For anyone who is in service of receiving or being a guide, allow yourself and the other to be seen without the label that the person is considered to be. Healing occurs only when we create room for it.

This is a beautiful way to expand perspectives and remember the holistic individuality of each human. I know that each body has all this wisdom already within all this knowledge.

So here we have again the yin and yang, the manifested and unmanifested. The physiological and the mental is intertwined and the outlines that are the path of harmonious symbiosis.

I always like the romanticism to see how mental manifests in the physiology and physiology in the psychological behaviour. What I think is very interesting is that many mental illnesses include a degenerative behaviour towards oneself. As you know our cells listen. As soon as we start an identification with an illness or condition the cells start to turn from giving their best for regeneration into degeneration and as we learned with the identification with the illness it therefore harms the body. Here I suggest to recognise how the mental manifests in the physiological. The funny thing is that the physical can be decaying through the naturally given lifespan plan and as well through noceboes and beliefs. But if we live from intuition we gain the opportunity to not let mental convictions, behaviours or patterns guide our general well-being. Even if the physiological body decays there is the opportunity to invite it to just be however the body wants to be and from there on act intuitively as our cells are always drawn to constant evolution without any forced effort.

# 47.  Anxiety

Going beyond fear is often used as a description to just
challenge the fear. Anxiety has its roots with the
meaning 'to choke'. I feel that is a beautiful description
that actually is quite accurate when comparing it to how
I experienced anxiety and anxiety attacks. What happens
if we break the habit of fear just by diving into it without
judging what would or could happen if we turn from
fearful behaviour into loving behaviour?

The physiological body is like a radio that transmits the
quality of our emotional state. It can't be separated
because there has never been such a thing and there is no
such thing as separation or disconnection between the
body and the mind. To express as human both are just
separated for intellectual reasons even if they are
actually one. As we have seen, beliefs shape our
perspective on life. So thoughts that bring us in a state
that's not arising from our intuition can be seen as
degenerative substances. They work degenerately on
physical and emotional health. They are actually what

could be called emotion-caused free radicals. Let's see what example anxiety brings with its expression.

Anxiety is a normal emotional response to a threat or potential threat. But if our cells couldn't metabolise moments which marked us with traumata the understanding of the difference between what a threat is and what is an unbalanced threat response of my body can be developed with intuition training. Here it is important to see that each body has a natural response to threat that is wired within the body and a response to threat that we label as threat through experiences and belief systems that get to express themselves the same way. Emotional experiences that are not metabolised lead to general health problems.

So whenever we experience an overwhelming emotion that we sense as negative and very persistent this emotion lowers the receptivity of nutrients within our cells and changes the harmonious balance of nutrients, pressure and structure within the body which creates oxidative stress. So anxiety, stress, depression, fear and other emotions and experiences like panic attacks or obsessive compulsive disorder interfere with our natural ability to handle oxidative stress and then stress out the body's emotional and physiological metabolism of experiences.

Oxidative stress is always present in depression anxiety. You can imagine negative thought patterns really as a degenerative pill which has an important role in the so-called genesis of anxiety.

This is another great example how the physical body responds and how it is directly wired with our beliefs. It is another invitation from my side to let what human science shows us to sink in. Even if a peaceful state of mind doesn't require any explanation, if you are taking this as an opportunity to get more intuitive allow yourself to get to know your individual physical expression. Let's go further; so oxidative stress occurs through free radicals.

So what are free radicals? Those free radicals and oxidants have a dual role on one side both can be toxic and as well beneficial. They work as harmful or helpful to the body.

They mostly derive from normal cell metabolisms or from our external world like environmental factors, medication and pollution. When the balance is disturbed which occurs when the body can't metabolise or transform those they start to they accumulate. And then the body starts to generate this phenomenon which is called oxidative stress. This process of oxidative stress which is the not metabolisation and transformation of stored physiological and psychological trauma creates physiological conditions. This can be from development of chronic and degenerative illnesses like cancer, fast ageing, autoimmune disorders, rheumatoid arthritis, cardiovascular conditions and neurodegenerative conditions.

Our beautiful body has many mechanisms to metabolise oxidative stress and produce antioxidants which could be seen as the guards that protect us from those conditions. The best sources that the body uses to synthesise antioxidants are fresh, plant-based foods and supplements which are naturally produced.

Knowing now that we can help the physiological body to decrease free radicals by creating beneficial emotions that work as antioxidants and food that as well can be an electron donor we understand why the intuitive system of the body always chooses the best option for the individual evolution. Remember here that intuitive living is the portal to a life in total peace, health and freedom of mind. Your intuition will always lead you to have all that is needed.

Those so-called free radicals could also be defined like any molecular species which can independently exist and has an unpaired electron within the atomic orbital. An unpaired electron leads to certain common properties which are shared by most of the radicals. Many of those radicals are highly reactive and very unstable. As they can donate an electron or as well receive an electron from other molecules they behave as reductants or oxidants.

Generally radicals can attack through attacking macromolecules and be a cause of cellular damage and the disruption of homeostasis. Free radicals target not only lipids and proteins but as well nucleic acids which are the ones that mostly get attacked. So to make it short and simple a radical can be an oxygen or a carbon atom with an unpaired electron which is unstable and highly charged. Free radicals are missing electrons and can make the body and the mind degenerate faster than natural.

To support the body we would need to find some electron donors or antioxidants besides fresh, unprocessed plant-based foods from the soil we walk on but only if we walk barefoot. When we connect to the ground with our skin Mother Earth gifts us with literally life energy that supports our natural self-regeneration gift. Nature provides it all for free. Earthing and often called grounding as well is about the skin contact with the earth. Walking barefoot in nature nourishes the whole body and for me I sense how it enhances my physiological health. Walking in the forest or on grass is what nourishes me intensely. I always could see how the energy of the earth would enter through the ground into my body. It always makes me feel more alive as well after a lightning through the air or in lakes, rivers, springs and the sea. So how is that possible? The electrically conductive connection of the body with the surface of the earth actually produces antioxidative effects on the holistic health. There is a fascinating connection to lower processes of inflammation in the body while connecting to the earth. This intimate touch when 'kissing the earth', as Thich Nhat Hanh would say, not only affects our immune responses but as well triggers wound healing. It works preventatively, and as we now know can support in treatment of autoimmune conditions and chronic inflammatory conditions.

Interesting is that while grounding and measuring the organism there were differences in the concentrations of leukocytes, cytokines and other molecules which are involved in the inflammatory response. Grounding or earthing as well affects chemical factors which are related to inflammation in the body.

Earthing or grounding has other benefits as well: one is reducing pain. Besides that it alters the numbers of circulating a specific type of white blood cell important to fighting off infections and lymphocytes which are an important part of the immune system as well. It can prevent or even help the body with silent inflammations.

This all happens because the body receives free electrons from the earth and—if you can recall what a free radical has? Yes, an unpaired electron—Earth donates the electrons to the body and therefore they can have antioxidant effects. Other astonishing side effects that walking barefoot has is it supports to normalise the day-night cortisol rhythm and reduces stress.

Earthing is a free and natural health-boosting practice that helps with chronic inflammation. Remember, when I push myself or others down I am in inflammation too. I see how nature nourishes our conscious experience by feeding us with non-intellectual information. Earthing and for me generally nature contact recharges our energy level and it is very effective to recharge our physiology with energy. While you go through all the contents and set yourself a reminder that it can be believed, in the end it's just a belief. As if I believe I know my intuition knows best and I gift my conceptual mind with the intellectual understanding of why I behave the way I do.

Walk as if you are kissing the Earth with your feet.

—Thich Nhat Hanh, Peace Is Every Step: The Path of Mindfulness in Everyday Life

Physical health can be a key point for mental health and on the other side mental health can impact the physical state. So looking into how mental health is described by the Princeton University: mental health is a 'psychological state of someone who is functioning at a satisfactory level of emotional and behavioural adjustment'. Do we need to be functioning at a satisfactory level? Often we would rather listen to a concept of health than the wisdom that's beyond concepts. So we know that drugs, alcohol, over medication and foods low in antioxidants can decrease the general health and increase conditions and inflammation, which, if you remember, impacts the mental state as we start to press ourselves and others down.

Just a little elaboration on alcohol before I go further in accumulation in the cells. I just want to mention alcohol as it is one of the most addictive drugs that is being abused by lots of humans on the planet. A little fact on alcohol: in already five minutes the ethanol molecules enter the bloodstream which are easily absorbed mostly through the small intestine and stomach and after gets distributed to all organs, including our precious brain. The liver has lots of work to be able to process one standard drink; it needs one hour. In a Harvard Health Publishing article they stated 'moderate drinking linked to decline in thinking skills'. Do I think drinking is essential for a life that's lived in freedom and peace? I don't think so. But what I sense is that if I lose control of thinking then it is that I may suffer. For me even the

365

most moderate amount of alcohol can be harmful if it occurs several times a year. On the other hand, my granny always said the greatest artists were wine drinkers. I want to make this point clear as this question arises often. Alcohol can be used as a medicine, yes, accompanied by doctors. Drinking consciously may change the experience of alcohol. Thus once you connect totally to all parts of your body you are able to produce any drug yourself and don't need the cellular side effects of alcohol. The natural gift of interacting intuitively and instinctively is slowed down. Alcohol may cause reflexes to become slow and coordination issues to arise which goes to our speaking center. Neurotransmitters and nerve cells are affected as soon as the alcohol crosses the blood brain barrier. It leads to general depression in the central nervous system which means lowering the quantity of sent signals from the brain to the rest of the body. Most people who consume alcohol heighten their risk of injuries as the body's structure of molecule interaction changes. Personality changes, brain damage, sexual impotence which includes reduced fertility, problems with concentration and memory, sleeping difficulties, cancers, liver conditions, heart conditions and stomach ulcers are related to alcohol consumption.

When we do not process our thoughts, emotions and experiences we start to accumulate those energies and they get stuck within our cells. As well the byproduct of those experiences if we don't metabolise them is an overwhelming accumulation which supports the DNA, lipids and proteins not to regenerate, transform or be metabolised but to be oxidised by free radicals which then is often responsible for an early aged brain or age-related neurodegenerative disorder. There can be other factors as well, external and genetics. For me, energy that is not metabolised only can harm me if I didn't learn to metabolise it. What I sense is that everything has its right to be at the place it is. As in the back of the concept of what should and what shouldn't, there sleeps the source of wisdom itself.

So can intuition be trained? Yes, and what does it do? It deepens our emotional intelligence. So what is this emotional intelligence? It is be ability to cope with the demands in the environment. It is the ability to know what wisdom the emotions and feelings in the body can behold and make us understand how to integrate what they want to show us. It seems to have an important role in general health as the so-called emotional intelligence is involved as well in biological factors in the regulation of oxidative and antioxidant processes. And in addition having a reduced activity of the enzymatic antioxidant processes seems to come with impairment of cognitive performances. So the brain works not in its individual, natural-given harmony and these lower cognitive functions are at the peripheral blood levels and the central nervous system. This shows that knowing how to live with the individuality of each body enables to understand the cellular wisdom it offers.

It is crucial to not separate psyche from physiology. No distinction can be made between psyche and physiology; one can even reflect the other. To turn it around and see it from the other side, that emotional intelligence is altered through antioxidant levels, would that be a thing? If I know that inflammation, stimulating substances and drugs alter the way that I experience emotionally reality, I can choose consciously from which perspective I decide to use and which reaction I identify with or not. Is an emotional intelligence something that should be achieved? After my later experience I started to look differently at my body. I could sense that there were so many wires reorganised in my whole system. Always when the question comes up or the urge of achieving it I feel that we do not need to add something to us but yes, metabolise and let the energy of the moments that we have experienced transform.

Whenever I connect to the deepest source within me I hear that it is not a privilege to live in freedom and peace but it is trainable in the third dimension if we have such an open heart to integrate all three forces. The mind, the body and the essence not only of the self but of all that be perceived as others. As if we have lower emotional intelligence we also have a lower spiritual and physiological immune system. You may recall that free radicals damage in a not balanced state the physiology and may support a mind that is disordered as well. Even cardiovascular and inflammatory conditions like the pull down (depression) or cataracts and cancer have a strong correlation to high amounts of free radicals which couldn't be transformed. On the other hand, remember that antioxidants support to lower damages that may occur to tissues. I speak here only about natural antioxidants that nature provides with fresh, biophoton-high and plant-based foods. When you start to include into your food choices functional foods which have a high level of antioxidants you may support your body's general health. Please be aware that the intuitive system of knowing what has most value for your cells may be trained with the intuitive reset method for general health.

So the conclusion is that free radicals are of crucial importance to human health when maintained in a low quantity, or better said, the balanced quantity. As we know they are a part of the process to synthesise specific cellular attributes and to be utilised from the body to fight pathogens which are trying to invade the body. An amazing fact is that our phagocytes, our protection cells, actually synthesise and store free radicals. They eat what we don't need and keep what we may need. So they keep those free radicals and then they can release them when invading pathogenic visitors in the body to have the power to destroy them. That's so sci-fi, I can't get enough of that. Interesting, isn't it?

I would love you to let this sink in with a deep breath; science is wisdom that came to paper. We all have the intuitive knowledge about how to care about this wonderful vehicle that we use to express ourselves. We all know how to be whole, how to be holy, we just have to allow ourselves to access it.

# 48. Intuitive Reset Method for Improving General Health

Does your intuition always send you to the bakery, donut bar or fast food restaurants? Okay, super funny topic: let's take a look to see why we often rather choose to be compulsive than intuitive. How do we get back to the intuitive selection that nourishes our cells and supports them with their regenerative work? Here I will explain how to practise understanding the cellular wisdom with the tool of the intuitive reset method for improving general health. It is a method that supports intuitive eating habits. Why intuitive eating? Because i sense that it is crucial for general health.

'Research on intuitive eating has increased in recent years. Extant research demonstrates substantial and consistent associations between intuitive eating and both lower BMI and better psychological health.'
Relationships between intuitive eating and health

indicators: literature review. Van Dyke N1, Drinkwater
EJ2. NCBI


Intuition for me is to practise the practice of unpractising
so that I can understand my beliefs and listen to the inner
wisdom. Science for me is the practical guide and
application to find methods to integrate wholeness on a
conceptual level in the modern life. To be conceptual it
would be lead rather by our thoughts and mind than from
the intuitive wisdom. So it would be more theoretical
than experiential. When I practise my conscious and
unconscious convictions, then it is when studies can
serve as the wonderful conceptual understanding of how
cellular wisdom would behave and then to use it
intellectually for general health. I see science as a tool to
theoretically understand how the body works in the 3-D
world. It is the development of the theoretical ground
principles of cellular knowledge. Intuition is the
translation of the wisdom that our cells carry. Intuition
always leads to health, freedom and peace. If I follow
my intuition and not just beliefs, acquired knowledge
and ideas, then miracles happen. This is an invitation to
be recognising impulsive or compulsive behaviour.


If science is a development that came out of intuition
and science says that donuts are not healthy, why would
I get cravings of donuts in the supermarket?

Well, depending on what food we give the body, it allows different bacteria to reproduce more or less in our digestive tract. The messages and signals that are sent to our brain via the microbiome also control eating behaviour. This communication between the digestive system and the mind can be the physiological reason for compulsive choices. Not only do the gastrointestinal tract and the brain communicate through the nervous system, but they also communicate through hormones and as well through the immune system. This connection is called gut-brain axis, and it consists of bidirectional communication between the central and the enteric nervous system which is connected to the cognitive and emotional centers of the brain with peripheral intestinal functions. Its essential to recognise the importance of the gut microbiota in influencing our behaviour and interactions. Microorganisms in the gut help regulate the body's immune response. Should we not be aware of this, the microbiome regulates our eating habits.

Malnutrition caused by incorrect food combination, overeating of processed foods low in biophotons and the metabolic leftovers can fog our sixth sense, otherwise called intuition. This disturbs the symbiosis with the beneficial bacteria, the harmonious balance with the organism, and leads to the suppression of the immune defence because the intestine is the largest immune organ in the human body, in which 80% of the immune system is localised. The brain-gut axis even takes part in the process of regulation of brain chemistry and influencing neuro-endocrine systems associated with stress response, anxiety and as well with our memory. Integrating wholeness through an intuitive lifestyle is the key that enables health. A conceptual food choice can be a theoretical ground principle rule to follow, thus intuition for me has a knowledge that is still beyond what we can intellectually understand.

So what does conceptual or theoretical food choice look like? I can go to the supermarket and through all the essential conceptual things I would like to integrate. For example, I can choose food that supports my current goal when it comes to losing weight, or foods that rejuvenate, detoxify the body, and foods that increase productivity or creativity. The other option is to choose to eat intuitively; then I go to the supermarket and decide from my body's pendulum.

Let's come back again to the donuts. What if my pendulum wants to get married with the donuts, how can it be that my intuition necessarily wants donuts even if science tells me I shouldn't? Everyone has the gift of being able to feel what food is right for them. The intuition that is not compulsive, free of beliefs and dogmas gives me access to the body's cell knowledge of what foods are the best for me. Reasons why I cannot understand my cellular wisdom could be my beliefs about nutritious values or a stuffed interstitium, intracellular accumulations, which could as well be accumulations of heavy metals in the adipocytes also known as fat cells, drug residues, and a calcified pineal gland. Cells store traumas and emotional experiences as well which also play a role in choices that are theoretical rather than intuitive. We can train the intuition in a way that we sense experientially what science reveals theoretically.

So even with trauma and all that stuff stuck in our body is there a possibility to send the body again to the intuitive approach? Of course … So how do I get to the intuitive reset method for improving general health? It's easy … Fresh, organic vegetables and fruits help the body with detoxing. Sounds simple? It actually is even easier than it sounds. It is essential that the body detoxes, this happens when I feed it with fresh, unprocessed, healing plant- based food, not if I consume again lots of clogging food or clogging beliefs. Go to the supermarket and pick four fruits or vegetables that science revealed as healthy. Then pick it up and feel what your body is most attracted to, and it will be the healing plant your cells choose. Now for the next three to seven days, take a fruit or vegetable and consume only this for several days. After three days, the microbiome has already adjusted. Peace does not depend on physiological experiences.

After I have chosen intuitively between fresh fruits and veggies, I can also inform and investigate what amazing health benefits those that I have chosen bring. The knowledge of health benefits strengthens the self-healing powers. So I can use the efficiency of the healing plant that I have chosen and use it like a practical and potent tool to intensify healing. The mind is continually the creator of reality.

Another method that I like to use is to abstain from solid foods and consume liquids only.

Fasting is one of my favourites to set the intuition back to 100%. Like above explained it usually takes me one to three days to see which patterns are compulsive and what is intuitive eating. Fasting not only regenerates the intuitive body knowledge but strengthens the immune system. It helps the body to detoxify and through the process of autophagy fasting works as a tool to metabolise misfolded proteins, organelles, and helps as well to metabolise stuff that is stuck in the fat cells or intercellular space and recycles them.

Intuition is life with an open heart. Integration of everything we are. If you decide to integrate intuitive nutrition, you will benefit from a new body feeling in a short time. You will be clearer in your thoughts and experience the day more consciously. It's a lovely way to cleanse from the old and make space to experience what is now. Your body is your most loyal friend and will guide you through your life in the most honest way; don't hesitate to integrate its knowledge. Don't forget that the weather is never the same: one day it's sunny, the other day cloudy, the next day rainy. Some days we have it all in one. Views and perspectives on life shape the experience of being human from physiological, emotional and social health. Intuition shapes views and perspectives into love and as we all know it is love that cures.

As long as you think that the cause of your problem is 'out there'—as long as you think that anyone or anything is responsible for your suffering—the situation is hopeless. It means that you are forever in the role of victim, that you're suffering in paradise

—Byron Katie, Loving What Is: Four Questions That Can Change Your Life

# 49. Forgiveness

If there is no path perceived to forgiveness it is a defence mechanism. It is the only identified sense of self.

... when the me thinks it knows the you, then it is when the me and you is created.

When the I forgets who is the you, then the I no longer distinguishes between both and integrates the one who thinks in me and you and the presence beyond that. That's forgiveness. It created the we.

All that happens to us and is perceived through the egoic identity becomes meaningless and all that is meaningless becomes a miracle.

Allow yourself to just look at whatever is in this very moment what you are perceiving with your two eyes and see reality. Feeling your body is feeling reality.

Nothing really ever happens the way imagination shows us. Whatever imagination is showing us is not reality. Your two eyes seeing this very moment is the only reality. As you allow yourself to do nothing but unpractised beliefs you will enlighten every thought and belief that clouds your feelings. Take those beliefs and convictions as a guide to heal what isn't healed yet.

I'm simply saying that there is a way to be sane. I'm saying that you can get rid of all this insanity created by the past in you. Just by being a simple witness of your thought processes. It is simply sitting silently, witnessing the thoughts passing before you. Just witnessing, not interfering, not even judging, because the moment you judge you have lost the pure witness. The moment you say 'this is good, this is bad' you have already jumped onto the thought process. It takes a little time to create a gap between the witness and the mind. Once the gap is there, you are in for a great surprise, that you are not the mind, that you are the witness, a watcher. And this process of watching is the very alchemy of real religion. Because as you become more and more deeply rooted in witnessing, thoughts start disappearing. You are, but the mind is utterly empty. That's the moment of enlightenment. That is the moment that you become for the first time an unconditioned, sane, really free human being.

—Osho

If we follow the forgiving guidance of intuition we recognise that we are the ones that we need to forgive. It's feeling one's own essence and pureness. That's what this book is all about. Experiencing reality and seeing how kind and beautiful it is. 'Reality is harsh.' Does that feel like this is coming from your intuition? Reflect on it. let this sink in 'Reality is harsh'.

This book guides through practice to use the intellect as a gate to reach the essence of oneself. Remember that this practice has the opportunity to let you live from a place that doesn't need to constantly use intellect to be guided, it is a practice to live from your core energy. Living from the gut to realise that our perception shapes the world and that we can expand this beautiful human experience from a mind that loves to cage into the mind that opens cages, closes cages, creates cages and dissolves cages. All patterned thoughts can be opened up and from there on see reality and what really exists in front of our two eyes. It allows to unlearn the convictions and remember the essence within the only moment that is the portal to healing the now. It helps to not judge what we think is happening, what could and hasn't happened, and what is happening right now. It helps us to just flow with whatever experience we might go through. It makes us love. The quality of thoughts and feelings change from labelled ones to clear ones.

If I don't know I have a mind that cages me through beliefs in my experiences then I don't know I'm caged through my mind and that there is more than what holds me back from being myself. So this mind makes all external experiences responsible for the way that I feel and if we live from intuition this same mind is a pointer to make me aware that it isn't the external world that created my experiences. It is my thoughts and beliefs that I reflect on others and we just haven't been aware of it. This is the game changer to realise forgiveness: from sending the guilt to others recognise the guilt from oneself and forgive thyself and forgive others.

Once living from intuition there is no reason to forgive because the connection to our essence doesn't judge. But it is the opportunity to recognise that guilt and forgiveness are created by myself. Recognise that every human, including me, is doing whatever he is doing because we think it is right. Intuition clears the vision and shows the innocence of everyone. All that ever happens if we suffer is imagination. Living intuitively is taking all that's stuck within us away and forgive for whatever has been and forgive for whatever might come. Every experience that's filtered through beliefs is a mirror and pointer to all the love that is hidden behind the sciences. Every dogmatic belief is like a heavy weight: it can create suffering, it is lifted by not believing and not practising beliefs and seeing reality as it is. If there is no weight there is no pain or suffering that will take away our opportunity to transform what we experience. There a lot of space to experience, embrace, create and be the source of existence. It is the honouring of emotions.

Forgiveness is often seen as forgiving what the other has done to oneself but from the core perspective there is nothing to forgive because whatever the other has committed and made me uncomfortable was me making me uncomfortable. How does that make sense? My beliefs make me think the other has to act in a way that I think he should. If he ever should act in a different way the egoic identity gets triggered because the egoic identity loves to fight if something wants to push us into reality. So me forgiving you for what you have done creates hierarchy which is always segregating. But if I just forgive me and you for any judgement it is a way to heal the past.

Forgiveness is realising there was and is nothing to forgive. It allows us to take away all tags that we plug on another. If we take those tags away we allow the other and ourselves to be seen from our essence. Be seen the way we are in this moment and not the way that we have acted once and therefore we should act the same way. Did you ever see a cloud rain the exact same way another cloud rained? Did you ever have a day that repeated itself the same way? Nature is a great gate to inspiration when it comes to forgiveness. Looking deep, there is nobody to forgive, it's only the egoic belief system that wants to prove the other wrong and the self right. It is acting out a belief.

Forgiveness means that nothing happened in this moment, it happened in the imagined past. That doesn't mean it didn't happen or that there aren't things happening that can hurt our feelings or even physical pain. It just gives us the opportunity to experience whatever might happen without fearing it. Everything is dependent on whether I believe my thought or I reflect on reality. It shows again that our world is shaped the way that we perceive it. If we only believe our thoughts we perceive it in a caged and limited way. If we live from intuition we can perceive all stages. Living intuitively is the way to live beyond beliefs and create peace, freedom of mind and health; thus if you want one of those to amplify your life's quality you may lose it and be running in the back of a concept.

And so I tell you, every kind of sin and slander can be forgiven, but blasphemy against the Spirit will not be forgiven. Anyone who speaks a word against the Son of Man will be forgiven, but anyone who speaks against the Holy Spirit will not be forgiven, either in this age or in the age to come. Make a tree good and its fruit will be good, or make a tree bad and its fruit will be bad, for a tree is recognised by its fruit.

—Matthew 12:31-33 NIV

# 50. Intuitive and Emotional Intelligence

For me intuitive and emotional intelligence can be increased and relearned through practice and lifestyle changes; here I want to elaborate whether a plant-based diet that is a part of lifestyle changes can help the body to increase even general intelligence. Why plant based? You probably have heard about the power of healing plants so I want to ask if you ever heard about healing pizza or healing fast food in general? Me neither.

What I found while researching was that it seems that generally higher scores for IQ in childhood seem to be a factor which increases the likelihood in adult life of being a vegetarian. I found that very intriguing.

As we know excessive consumption of refined foods and saturated fat are not only associated with the risk of developing obesity which can be a main factor in developing cardiovascular conditions and diabetes but as well reduces the cognitive function, and supports dementia and cognitive decline. So yes, it is a potential risk factor when it comes to cognitive impairment development. Plant-based foods high in biophotones work here protectively and as we have seen emotional intelligence is as well a factor to be considered when it comes to general health.

Did you ever hear the sentence 'The apple doesn't fall far from the tree'? Hmm, I love this quote but what I love even more is the way Dr Michael Greger explains genetics, behaviour and disease relations. Often similar characteristics, symptoms and conditions are found to run in family members.

'The primary reason diseases tend to run in families may be that diets tend to run in families.'

I discovered this amazing quote by Dr Michael Greger in a talk he had at Google speaking about his book called *How Not to Die*. And the way I sense it the same takes over when it comes to behaviour.

So let's see what this research reveals about the relationship between general intelligence, emotional intelligence, stress levels and stress reactivity?

Stressful events that are overloading our system have damaging effects. The word damage comes from the Latin damnum 'loss, hurt'. I see this as a beautiful reflection and projection on how the physiology mirrors the psychological expression. For me, it is the I lost myself in life and the 'I' is hurting itself and others when the 'I' is stressed, and cumulative effects. On the other hand, stress as well has an cumulative effect. So cumulative holds its meaning in to heap, that indeed is the non-metabolisation and transformation of what I experience. When this happens then the energy starts to stock within the body and the mind. Generally stress has the power to work with our mental functions, from concentration, to learning and even attention and memory. Knowing the inner states of the individual expression of self as a skill helps one to handle whatever life brings without effort and without the practice of handling especially when it would come to acute stress and chronic stress. As the weather is never the same we as well daily have a different expression of the self daily. As well every entity has its individual, different intuitive stress-handling level. The better you understand your cellular inductive and individual wisdom the less stress you may experience. Something I found while researching more about this is that the so-called general intelligence had no significant correlation with the emotional intelligence which for me is a base for intuitive cellular understanding.

The better you connect to your intuitive wisdom you may more clearly sense what the physiological reactions are to stress and the coming mental or cellular beliefs of the biology. Long I was wondering why sometimes my physiology would react to other people's suffering like I was experiencing it. The understanding of being able to distinguish between the emotions of oneself and others while still sensing the connection and presence is crucial for individual and social health. Only when I understand what is mine and what happens to me, because my body has such a power of feeling and imagining, can I open myself up and metabolise it to transform all experiences into a wisdom source. The scientific term of emotional intelligence is very close to this intuitive wisdom, and it can be experienced only by unpractising one's beliefs. Those in the mind and those that are in the cells didn't get the chance yet to reveal what wisdom they offer. It is like meditation with all that is. Unfolding reality is for me personally the key point. Stepping out of imagination and gaining back the opportunity to see reality as it is.

A new hypothesis is proposed for a better understanding of the meditative mind. Meditation is an art of being serene and alert in the present moment, instead of constantly struggling to change or to become. It is an art of efficient management of attentional energy with total engagement (poornata, presence, mindfulness) or disengagement (shunyata, silence, emptiness). In both states, there is an experience of spontaneous unity with no sense of situational interactive self or personal time. It is a simultaneous, participatory consciousness rather than a dualistic, sequential attentiveness. There is a natural sense of well-being with self-understanding, spontaneous joy, serenity, freedom and self-fulfillment. It is where the ultimate pursuit of happiness and the search for meaning of life resolve. One realises the truth of one's harmonious being in nature and nature in oneself. It is being alive at its fullest, when each conscious moment becomes a dynamic process of discovery and continuous learning of the ever-new unfolding reality.

—Neuroscience of Meditation from
Vinod D. Deshmukh

# 51. Reality

So what is reality? Reality is what you are perceiving in this very moment with your two eyes. It isn't what's going to happen in one second or what happened a second ago. It just is what is perceived now. It may be an apparent reality as soon as it is experienced through the perspective on being sure how it was perceived. Indeed it is the opportunity to recognise once inner beliefs which shape what we think reality is. Often our sensory perceptions give us the power to experience the now and then the believing mind creates a romantic story around it.

Let's take a plane full of people. Every person in this plane has from each seat a different perspective and perception. Even if every person would once sit in all the other seats the perception would never be the same as in our individuality we experience all according to our psychological and physiological constitution. To be sure about something may often be filtering reality. The reality that I refer to is the one that is perceived in the given moment with the two eyes. Not one minute in the past not one minute in the future. It is using general term explanations without the story that the mind would apply as then it is that I know instinctively how to handle any situation with all the power that I'm individually gifted with.

If I look at an object and label it without the story I think I know about it I start to communicate with the essence of it. I leave space for the object to be as it wants to be in any given moment. For example, when I look at a rose I may be able to recognise and remember yes, the story of all that I have experienced or seen that involved a rose. Emotions, thoughts and ideas where and for what a rose may stand. If I look at the rose and see all the stories that my mind and cells offer me while looking at it I may experience the beautifully romantic or terrifying around it. Within those experiences and stories there is the source of existence. When I allow myself and the rose to be as we just came into existence I may utilise the wisdom that I gained in this life, integrate wisdoms that my cells carry and then sense life within all that's here. I give the rose as an object the chance to be whatever the rose wants to be in the next moment. So reality in my sleeping mind is what I think and belief is what I think it seems to be. Often there is no better proof of something being reality when we have seen it with our eyes. Thus know as soon as it has passed and the mind labels it with a story it is an imagination. We may utilise our imagination with the intention of curiosity and peace to deepen the arrival in the moment and use the wisdom of the past for future effortless behaviour.

There are three sciences in the study of man. The first is the Science of Ordinary Knowledge; the second is the Science of Unusual Inner States, often called ecstasy. The third, which is the important one, is the Science of True Reality: of what lies beyond these two. Only the real inner knowledge carries with it the knowledge of the Science of Reality. The other two are the reflections, in their own form, of the third. They are almost useless without it

— The Chariot

# 52. Cell-awareness and Cell-Attention

'We can move from autopilot to aware' is a sentence I heard at the at google developed SIY program. Which for me means being connected to the cells. Seeing if my attention is within my cells and if i have awareness of my cells and where my attention wanders. We all have the mysterious and powerful capacity of awareness and attention. Exploration of these through practice helps us become more familiar with different mental processes and metabolize old stuck things from within us. For my better cellular understanding i love fasting as an 'dedicated practice' to unpractice consumption. I feel how it supports me in better understanding my cellular needs and connect to my cellular awareness.

When I first started fasting. In the first day of my fast I recognised that the hunger I was feeling wasn't by my belly it actually was constantly my mind telling me that I needed something to eat. So funny thing, after 24 hours of fasting I didn't have any more of those cravings and I could recognise how my thought patterns on food would change when I was having conversations about situations that normally related to food consumption. Like having a good conversation was always physical consumption as well. It showed me how often I would just consume not only food and drinks but also information that my intuitive system didn't even ask for; it was more of a kind of program that I had within me. This helped me to recognise and be familiar with different mental processes. When I was breaking my fast and drank my first cup of green tea I was amazed how it impacted the way that my body reacted and the most amazing thing was from there on I could have different physical reactions but be aware of them developing Cell-awareness. Before I didn't even recognise that not only my thoughts but yes, all that enters my body impacts the wonderful vehicle I live in. Fasting gives me support in having a clearer Cell-Attention.

To understand how the gut and the brain communicate and can even make us feel anxiety, anger, sadness and other feelings we must look a little at the brain/ gut connection. What we know is that the brain has a direct link to affect our digestive tract even before we eat. Just the thought of ingesting something may release the stomach juice before food even gets there. This connection as well goes in the other direction. If your microbiome or intestine is troubled the communication to the brain may not work at its best. So a stress that comes from the mind, depending on which thoughts we consume, may stress the digestive tract and stress from the intestine, depending on what we ingest into our body, has the power to cause anxiety, depression and stress. Often there might not even be a physiological reason to find but it's experienced. And it is almost impossible to heal a distressed digestive tract without a holistic view that includes the states of stress and emotion.

Not only from the ancient ones, our personal experiences, but yes, as well from science, we know that we think, do and pay attention to changes in our mental experience and physiology.

The mental and the physical are linked.

Living intuitively is the update to live together in peace on this planet.

As you have understood it already, your thoughts are very powerful; we are creators. Everything we speak and pronounce and what we pay attention to creates this moment. In the beginning was the word.

Remember how beliefs shape perspectives? Whatever we think today and whatever we expect to happen will be reality in the next moment. Whenever we are in fear, anger, suffering, sad, against something, whenever we fight something then we believe our convictions and are not nourished by reality. We are nourished by negativity. Every word you read or hear will touch your cells.

Think about what you want your cells to be touched with. Knowing that we store knowledge and information within our whole system, feel free to go to your core and select from your essence the books you read, the media you consume and the people you are surrounded by. Living intuitively is living 'cellfully.' Do not be fooled by news and negative imagery; nothing that takes your joy away is ever reality. Never.

A couple of years ago I went to the Munich film academy. What I learnt was acting connected me with my mental experience and linked it to make me more aware of what cellular attention is. After reading several scripts and then going into the character to act the way the personality and beliefs of those characters were described, my body started to produce the same physiological experience as if I was living it. So as it really felt physiologically draining or happy and excited even after the act was finished, sometimes I would even get physically sick. In one of the characters I was a young brother that just experienced the death of his and his sister's parents. The thing is, the sister normally would drive them to their shop, this time she didn't because she was running late for her presentation. 'My sister' was amazed and happy because she got accepted with a scholarship from a university. In the moment when I came back from the hospital and was told that both had passed away she was already back home and she ran to me excited and hugged me happily and told me about how happy she was to finally sign the papers for the university. It was such a painful experience to drop her out of her happiness and try to talk to her because she was so excited that she wouldn't listen. So my role was to 'wake her up' to what had just happened. I experienced such physiological and emotional pain during this scene. I was amazed by what happens when I do not metabolise what the mind thinks is real, how it becomes real in the physiology. My body was shaking, my head was hurting, my heart felt broken. So when the scene was over I couldn't get directly out of the character; the pain increased seconds after the act for more than a couple of minutes. Even though I knew that it was because I used the practice of acting to identify with the beliefs of my personal story that I suffered, intellectualising wasn't helping the experience in this moment but yes, to feel the presence behind the act.

If you think you know it for sure then it is a fragment of the experience that is offered to you.

—Gita Chaudhuri, Psychologist

Then from nowhere I felt like my body was doing this on purpose as it believes what I think. I felt the flow of being and doing, being able to live the romanticism and sensing the presence behind it. It's hard to describe it. It sounds funny but then when I felt the hormones in my body decreasing I heard something within myself speaking and showing me in a guiding way that the only thing that is ever real is what I see with my two eyes right now in front of me. I really saw it so clearly. I had learned more about how the body and mind are best friends and their relation can prove reality or disprove it. In having this call to look at reality I felt like my body just pushed subconsciously an exit button where I was able to recognise that suffering is imagination created by what I say, think and believe, and as well not only for me, but for everyone else. So all that I was acting in this scene, all that I lived, all that I have ever lived. After this I became for the first time aware of how attention changes the biological processes and that we all could just with learning attention practices switch perspectives. The inner wisdom I got gifted from my later experience started to integrate the mind and knowledge like a building block to understand deeper the human experience. It supported me in understanding and being able to express intellectually what I have experienced. Getting out of thoughts into reality and through this moment gained freedom of mind. Especially from this experience I learned that practising attention and recognising what is happening in front of our two eyes is the best way for me personally to identify what is mental experience and what is reality.

With practice I can develop a deeper cell-awareness, of what is opening to my cells.

For instance, recalling the me in the plane to Hong Kong, waiting for my food, getting super upset because they forgot me and forgot to serve me and they were not giving me attention when I asked about my meal. So from my point of view now this was the egoic identity that was fighting with what is. I wasn't listening to my intuition, just hearing my mind. If I went back in time and would be listening to my intuition, it would be empathic understanding, non-judgemental and I would be in peace knowing I'm actually not starving, I'm just here sitting and will be pleased to get my food and if nt i will not die—a super neutral thought.

The aim of sharing all those experiences is to show how emotions have a physiological basis that leads us to cellular wisdom. Attending to physiological signals and integrating them helps us become more aware of our emotional state and intuitions, and supports decision making. It helps to see when the angel or the devil on the shoulder wanna paint reality more romantic or dramatic. When the I is identified with one of both the harmony is lost. So this was happening to me, I had created a life in a apparent future world. Which clouded the wisdom of intuition as I would learn at my last trip to Hawaii.

So on this trip to Hawaii, actually before leaving, I had constantly a pain in my left part of the breast. I saw something changing while travelling already in the way that my energy was flowing. I didn't give it that much attention, even if I knew that the body never gives you signs without a reason I just was so taken by the idea of creating something new. I was living in my apparent world in the mind. As I worked the last years with holistic health and knew that the breast stands for living truth from the heart, I couldn't find where I wasn't living from my heart. I had the imagination that living at a beautiful place is living from the heart. I always base my decision making on the trust to my intuition as long as it is not clouded by my convictions. So in this moment when the pain in the breast started was funnily the moment I decided to travel to Hawaii. Calling back i have seen when my intuition was telling me it's fine, you can follow your heart. I couldn't understand at that moment what was meant. A little later i will expand on the spiral that occured when i arrived in Hawaii and how i use it as a source of wisdom.

Intuition for me is the guide that leads us to inner wisdom that creates always freedom of mind, health and peace. For me, intuition is never something that would make me feel bad and make me experience something that I would consider bad. That would always be my beliefs and convictions that make me compromise to something. To compromise from a space that isn't led by intuition is losing intuition because beliefs, commitments and convictions that come from a space where we just act in a way we think we have to, that may arise from personal or social biases, cage us and take away the freedom of living intuitively.

So recalling the experience, when I started to travel and the pain in my breast increased and a breast tumour started to manifest I took a conscious moment to arrive within me, deeper and deeper, and I just got blown away when I realised that I was living, yes, from my intuition and from my heart with every stranger and friend, but with my family I still had some moments where I wasn't connected to the present moment and just doing what I thought was socially, ethically and romantically correct or I believed I had to do. This moment opened my two eyes again to see and look beyond my emotional state. Here it was a beautiful experience to recognise that it doesn't have to be a super present emotion to make us aware of how we can be more conscious and live connected on decision making. It neither the angel or the devil on the shoulder that speaks the language of intuition. I learned that the body as well is a wonderful portal to recognise if we decide from beliefs or from a space that is led by the physiological and emotional wisdom that arises through awareness of the present moment. When I don't live my inner truth and I'm not able to metabolise what I experience it starts to accumulate the untransformed energy into blockages.

Intuition is a teaching in a classroom of present tense.

—Dr Zumra Atalay

When i have Cell-awareness i get gifted with the tool to shift from what i think i am into something deeper than what i think. Investigation of emotions helps us to see that they are transient, change dependent on conditions, and not the whole story of who we are or what is absolutely true as there is only a fragmented truth experienced by the identity.


If I don't know I have a mind that cages me through beliefs in my experiences then I don't know I'm caged through my mind and that there is more than what holds me back from being myself and experiencing life's reality. So coming back to see what else happened to me and how I learned to see my patterns of response. During and after my water fast I learned when I had cravings that came from my mind to invite them, look at them and just let them be. Not believing what they are saying but yes, integrating them and recognising them. That impacted intensely the way that I looked at myself, remembering past experiences where I have not been that wise and compassionate about my life and others. So learning not to identify with the beliefs and convictions that the mind creates and as well to look behind those beliefs where I can really hear my intuition, really reframe my personal experience and understand where the intention was coming from—if it was me speaking from a space of openness or my egoic identity and the needs with it to compromise to a specific story on how I or others had to be. With connecting to myself and inviting me to myself I can alternate the way I feel and think about things. What we think is what we become.

How do I use my past as a source of wisdom to align with where my intuition is guiding me?

Alignment for me is living intuitively. It is being aligned with me as the observer of the angel and the devil. It is me connecting to reality. I experienced so often when I just believed my conceptual values and abilities, the ones I was identifying with, that I wasn't happy, energetic and had no drive to life that was effortless. There was always this sense of weight So by living intuitively, listening to what are my physical given abilities and what are values that nourish my cells and values that really are essential, I gained freedom of living the best way I could in this physical expression. So if I listen to my inside I just naturally act out and improve values and abilities that are beneficial for the physical and emotional state.

So at the same trip to Hawaii visiting Anita which just had moved there and we planned to create a new business together in beautiful Hawaii. I arrived and we both had been super inspired to create something for the future to live in Hawaii so we created this beautiful project of holistic living in Germany and had the plan to bring lectures and seminars that we were giving in Germany as well as bring it to other universities in the states and organisations. As soon as I arrived in the same day I had my first meeting with the vegetarian society and they invited us immediately after we spoke about our project to give a lecture on the topic of how to increase productivity through holistic living which made us feel humbled.

Anita had found a beautiful property close to Kapaa where she was living already with her husband for a couple of months. The way we always planned it, a house with a natural spring between the mountains with a fruit garden that carries so much fruit that we could never eat them all. It was the way i lived it in my imagination. Having nature providing us all that we need in a fantastic modern house, thousands of butterflies, flowers and trees that were hundreds of years old. All like we had ever planned it actually, totally like we had envisioned it. So before I came there Anita was mostly utilising her time to work with me on the articles about holistic living. She immediately started to work with me and we inspired each other to create a local business. In one week we created an organisation, had a couple of lectures planned and a business plan with a product line with which we planned to sponsor our lectures and articles as they were all pro bono. Sounded beautiful, as we had planned it.

Meanwhile, we were just working a couple of hours a day and her husband working from early in the morning till late in the night and having a hard time making money; he felt a little excluded. So one thing that we didn't think about was that how my granny always told me if passion is not within all about the same project that three is one too much. And actually that was what happened. We mostly used the mornings to work till lunch and the rest of the day we were spending to give counselling and personal meetings to give further knowledge we gained about holistic living. Every day as more conceptual I created the story of how my life in Hawaii looked and almost forgot to look with my two eyes; I felt that this wasn't what my inner guidance was showing me but rather the romanticism of the beautiful and creative mind. One evening I started to feel intense pain in my breast and I asked Anita to have a conversation. I told her what I was seeing in my body and that it was time for me to move and that I have chosen Tokyo as one of my supporters donated a plane ticket to me after a seminar that we gave at the vegetarien society of hawaii. We both understood the conceptual rather than intuitive Trojan horse that I had created.


That day when I decided to fly to Tokyo was the moment I knew I would write. I felt how the tumor decreased within a day. I recognized within mycells that i was aligned again. I didn't know when yet to travel and what to do in Tokyo but I knew it was time to share what power the mind has in hiding reality in filtering truth. Whatever obstacle will come looking with the inner wisdom it is only an obstacle for the mind and an invitation towards oneself. The greatest gift that I have ever received is to never suffer again as presence is there within and will point out when it's time to change direction. Like a cell knwoing its work, knowing its target. After this beautiful conversation with Anita and Ben (her husband) I felt that my body started to metabolise this concept as I allowed it to pass on. So in that transition i had 24 hours of a very strong fever, was very sick, I felt how my cells of the body would need a little more time to metabolise what had happened. I could sense myself passing away. I felt like my ideas needed to die. So they did, I left the concept, metabolised it by going into it and from that moment on that I decided to transform the concept and use presence and reality to be my guide I had this 24 hours of fever and being sick as a deep experience of waking up from a concept. I invited myself back to arrive through my two eyes in reality. I woke up once again from a dream and integrated reality by aligning myself with the deepest values instead of the idealistic thought values.

That moment I realised personally that presence and stillness doesn't require a healthy body as I was so amazingly present with every pain and heat and cold wave I experienced that I didn't even wait to let it pass. Before I knew it conceptually from working with others, now I have the wisdom accessed from within 'mycellf'. So I started my travel to Tokyo after my stay in Hawaii. As I arrived in Tokyo two of my close friends just moved to Tokyo, Tottie and Miguel. Two angels on earth. As I told Tottie that I just got to Tokyo she invited me to visit the google office and invited me to meet some of her friends and colleagues. Each of the encounters turned into an inspiring, warm-hearted intuition and wellbeing conversation where Tottie and I got the opportunity to express what was burning within us. Our full attention, combined with personal experiences, scientific findings and space to allow the other to be.

I arrived there and had several meetings, and each was so inspiring for me that I can't even describe it in words. The feedback that I got from Tottie was very heartwarming and inspired me even more to play around with the self-work practice journaling exercises that I love to create. Was the experience in Hawaii now a failure? All that I had experienced with Anita for nothing? I just can't believe the mind when it closes my cells. It was the opportunity to learn so much from my stay in Hawaii and Tokyo and the initiation to do more research, study more about individual physiology and psychology, and for the opportunity to see clearly that I have a tool that can create peace and freedom in a heart and mind that's open to see reality. It was the initial call to write this book which I could feel within me a while that I wanted to share. That I needed to share. This experience was a call to invite myself to mycells and listen to places I did not know about. It was learning to listen to the selectivity of my cells.

# 53. Can We Be Intuitively Selective?

Selectivity is a important part as intuition is in a way selective and not selective. My intention here is a simple example of selectivity and knowing how to serve oneself and others. I had a friend visiting me and we had a wonderful long conversation. Around 2 a.m. I still felt that she was enjoying the conversation the same way that I was and she had a hard time to get up and go home as well because the conversation was just so beautiful. So I told her that I love to talk to her and I'm going to need the rest of the night to recover for the next day. She said just a little more and I felt that my body was just exhausted and I understand that my body needs to be fit so that I'm able to serve and when I told her that she was insisting to stay still. So I tried to explain it in a different way: I said my body is like a radio, if the battery is empty the music is not understandable and that I'm sure that she wants as well to benefit the same way that we benefit from each other having a conversation. If I understand what my body values and what my cells are telling me I can access my inner voice more clearly and take it not really like a discernment but like a guide to remember how best to express my wisdom and have a more open perspective if I take care of this temple that I live in.

Living intuitively matters and it benefits yourself and others. Release your inner wisdom and create aha moments! Living intuitively consists of a series of practices. In this wonderful conceptual world practice can be the key practice or ingredient to unlocking our ability to unleash intuition. All practices and reflections here support you to understand how some parts of the physical body works and how some psychological states interact. It is cell-awareness. This is valuable to gain trust and insight in the efficacy of these practices. Experiences of those tools bring presence deepening and 'cellfulness' practices and reflect on the effect these have on the individuality. It is learning to be the mirror to oneself and others. It's a gate to learn cellular communication and support others effortlessly on their journey of getting intuitive.

The eye through which I see God is the same eye through which God sees me; my eye and God's eye are one eye, one seeing, one knowing, one love.

—Meister Eckhart, Sermons of Meister Eckhart

Compassion creates courage. Feeling our commonality with others, of struggle and longing and joy, enables a sense of courage and a natural motivation to be a part of a bigger picture.

Since I realised that I'm not only the image in my head I know that it doesn't matter what happens if I follow my inner voice, my intuition, and live through that with empathy and compassion; there is nothing to fear in this world anymore because there is nothing that can harm me if I can understand myself and even every other entity. All methods and practices in the book here support the development of those qualities.

Leading from the We. We all have the capacity to remember our deep interconnection with others, and to speak, act and lead from this place.

I had a beautiful moment with my parents in the car. Both were having an argument and discussing intensely. At one moment when they started to get really rude to each other I just took a deep breath and centered myself. Reconnected to my inner voice and I saw them as a reflection of me not wanting to accept the moment as it was. So what came out of me was Mum, Dad can we just pause a second, breath and realise that it is for all of us healthier, freeing and bringing peace when we just speak to each other with more love and kindness.

So this moment instead of separating me from them, telling myself how rude they are, judging them, I connected to my inner voice that is never judgemental and found the we in the noise. From that moment on we had three wonderful days together with love and kindness. Especially grateful for my parents that they gave me the opportunity to live on this planet and supported me with their love in moments where i could not love.

May the simplicity and complexity of life inspire me daily again.

# Last Word

Who am I? When we meet this question with space and curiosity, we may find ourselves and our values in a new light. When i allow the individuality of my intuition to take place i learn that there is a routine, which is like a road with a regular course while being always different. Living intuitively means to be within the cellf and being conscious about the always changing routine.

If I listen into myself and ask this question the first that appears is space,

with all and nothing inside.

It is dark and at the same time very bright.

It feels equal to all

beyond the borders of infinity.

If I would try to describe it in a expression I would be probably saying

I am.

Please allow yourself every morning to not remember who you and the other were yesterday.

Thank you.

Above all summits
it is calm.
In all the tree-tops
you feel
scarcely a breath;
The birds in the forest are silent.
Just wait, soon
you will rest as well.


—Wanderer's Nightsong, Johann
Wolfgang von Goethe

## ABOUT THE AUTHOR

Patrick Ehler was born in 1988 in Germany. After several years of autodidactism studying core concepts in life sciences, he took courses in the ground principles of biochemistry, physiology, genetics, and immunology at Harvard Medical School HMX. He acquired a deeper knowledge of biochemical constitutions, molecular biological structures and the core medical concepts of treatment and prevention of disease.

Since 2012, Patrick has been working intensively on recent studies on epigenetics, microbiology, salutogenesis, nutritional science and theories of intuitive nutrition that all together are the key to a healthy and joyful life. His work is about improving global health and global peace through cultivating intuitive choices.

Patrick teaches around the globe through personal encounters, individual counselling, seminars, lectures and contribute as an author at Paracelsus Naturopathic School publishing articles regarding holistic health.

To get in touch with Patrick Ehler, please visit *www.Patrick-Ehler.com*

43128546R00250

Made in the USA
Middletown, DE
24 April 2019